Peter Hoffmann

The Way We Were

Peter Hoffmann was educated at Hunters Tryst School Oxgangs Edinburgh and at Boroughmuir Senior Secondary School. After graduate and post-graduate studies in Edinburgh he worked for SCVS; the Scottish Episcopal Church; the private sector and thereafter mainly in local government as a chief officer.

Peter Hoffmann
The Way We Were

The Way We Were

'…Can it be that it was all so simple then
Or has time rewritten every line
If we had the chance to do it all again
Tell me, would we?
Could we?...'

Streisland

'Alison, my aim is true…'

Elvis Costello

Introduction

You can run.

But you can't outrun yourself.

This memoir is made up of extracts from my diaries from half a century ago. It captures a short-lived love affair between two Edinburgh teenagers back in the 1970s poetically recording a young man's joys and highs when the relationship with Alison was going well alongside writing of the lows, the despair and the misery of unrequited love.

She was mine for a season.

I'd longed after her for three years until that wondrous summer of 1975 followed by a cold hard dark and bitter winter.

She was fair of hair and fair of body. And of mind too. She was kind. She was full of life. She was a delight to be with. Perhaps if we hadn't fallen in love we'd still be friends today.

She came from a more affluent and different class to me. A middle class family with an architect father. They lived high up on the hills of Braid at Buckstone overlooking the Festival City. She attended the city's most privileged private school, Mary Erskine's.

I was brought up in neighbouring Oxgangs, a council scheme. Working class Oxgangs. As the crow flies, less than two miles away. Both children of the fresh and airy parts of the south of the city.

We never knowingly met until we took up athletics at Meadowbank Sports Centre which hosted the 1970 Commonwealth Games. It lit a fire amongst thousands of the city's young sportsmen and women.

Meadowbank was always much more than an athletics stadium. It was a Mecca. It was an alma mater for many of the city's young people. It brought many young loving couples together who if it hadn't existed would probably never have met. Their lives would have been forever different to what they are today. I've written on other forums of its centrality. And its place. And its importance in a generation's hearts and minds and memories.

We loved our athletics. We loved the camaraderie. We loved the social interaction. It was fun. Our dreams sustained us. They kept us attending evening after evening. To go training at Meadowbank throughout the four seasons of the year. Particularly so on wet, miserable, dark and cold winter evenings. What made a key difference for me was if the current love of my life was along. And that was more often Alison. If she wasn't there I would feel a bit flat. But if of a sudden she appeared how my heart lifted. It transformed and brightened the night. Not only would it give me that extra motivation to lift my performance there was the thought that I'd get the chance to speak to her. And in later years offer her a lift home. And give me a further hour in her company. All to myself. And when she became eighteen, for a short season, a lift back to Dunfermline College of P.E.

We were an integral part of that story. We cuddled up under a tartan blanket spectating in the depth of winter. We walked in harmony. Hand in hand. Around and around the running track after training on sun-kissed summer evenings when only a zephyr breeze blew.

That halcyon summer of '75 I finally won her heart. Thereafter came the onset of a bitter winter. An icicle pierced and shattered and broke my heart. Thereafter life was never quite the same again.

In the years leading up to that summer we fell in, then we fell out, then back in with each other, before separating for life. Or perhaps not. Perhaps we might yet meet one last time before that long journey into the dark night from which we never return. For a coffee. And a long chat. About those days of long ago. And of the days and the years since. And where life's journey thereafter took each of us.

As is the way of all failed lovers the question remains, if only we'd met sooner. Or more likely, met later.

But from the view in winter – the view from 45 winters - in some ways all that has happened in the years since is less vital to that year. And that season. When she was but eighteen. And I was nineteen. It still has the capacity to bring a tightness to my chest. How well I recall that summer of summers. Over half a lifetime ago. She was the first. The first real love of my life. And in that place in the world of firsts and lasts, there she remains.

As I write this memoir I'm moving toward being sixty-four in a few months' time.

Despite the cold facts I don't feel that old. I did a circuit and a run today. And after revisiting the journals and the diaries of my youth still I can project and place myself in to the shoes of that young man. Dazzled by the rays of summer. Blinded in the headlights of wintertime.

I was a boy of fifteen when I first saw this lovely vision of grace, beauty and transcendence. When I became a young man of nineteen I enjoyed the delights of her young love before the heartache and darker experience of life's harsh and bitter lessons visited upon me. Eventually we all have to pay for our pleasure. We'd never have mourned so deeply if we hadn't loved so gladly. As Burns so eloquently wrote 'If we'd never loved so dearly…'

In my heart of hearts I think that young man always knew that the dark harbinger of winter was coming for him. Winter is coming. The dark slayer was hovering in the wings. In the darkness. The destroyer of dreams. Standing in the gap in the curtain awaiting to emerge and scatter and spread a deep winter frost rather than the fairy dusts of the goddess of summer. And so began a season of ice.

But for those few heady months we cherished such moments from the goddess of summer's fruits. Her sweet favours and delights. The thrill of simply holding hands. Sweet kisses. Loving embraces. Taking the dog for a walk high up upon Arthurs Seat. Looking down on our precipitous city and across to the sunny, blowy and breezy views toward East Lothian. Down the east coast and the Firth of Forth to Gullane Sands. To where we trained hard on blissful and blessed off-season Sundays amongst our peers and friends. A part of the group. And apart from the group. And en-route home, stopping off at Musselburgh. Sitting out on the low wall. Enjoying our Luca's ice creams.

Rounding Dunsapie Loch we looked to the south. An endless future. To the ski slope of Hillend carved deep into Stevenson's Hills of Home. And to where we were brought up, she in the shadow of the Braid Hills and me in the lea of the Pentland Hills.

And as we walked under soft early autumn skies and zephyr breezes we laughed. She girlishly giggled.

I couldn't get enough of her. This vision and goddess incarnate. My heart's desire. We talked of our hopes. And our dreams. And our aspirations. And our plans and our futures. But of course God laughs at those who make plans.

But like every generation why wouldn't we? We were on the cusp of life. She stood at the entrance to life. We were at the start of life's journey and adventure. To the stars and beyond. We were full of hope and anticipation, naturally wishing to imbibe all of life's pleasures whilst we were young. After our boyhood and girlhood this was what awaited us. It was part of life's natural cycle. An apprenticeship for those short moments. Those few years that every generation experiences. The novelty and the thrill of being in love. And that it would last forever. Of course in our minds we knew it wouldn't. But in our hearts we were so immersed in the moment a small part of us thought it perhaps might just last. And we'd remain together. Not apart.

Ah, but time's winged chariot. This same rose that blooms today tomorrow will be dying. But for that summer of wonder we were very much alive with our youthful dreams and idealism. A golden age. There was a certain purity to our existence. And to our lives.

After a halted start I was gradually changing my life for the better moving toward fulfilling the triple crown of my heart's desires – to be in love and to be loved by a beautiful lady – and I was in rapture to her charms; my dream to become a world class athlete – not just an international athlete – in aiming for the stars I would reach atop of Olympus; and to continue to search out and explore academia and fulfil whatever potential I might have.

The future was mine. It was within touch. It was within my grasp. And similarly so for Alison. She was academically gifted. With good qualifications she'd won a treasured place at the finest and most prestigious P.E. college in the U.K. God, she was bright. And vivacious with it. She simply fizzed with life. She was fun. She was on the cusp of exploring life's many pleasures and joys. She loved Biba. She loved Bread. She loved me.

She was a good athlete. A national champion in the long jump. But she had the wisdom and self-awareness to realise that was all she might be. She could accept that achievement for what it was. I meanwhile continued to be a dreamer, she a realist and wise beyond her years. But kind and caring with that too. To tread carefully on my dreams. Well, as best and as carefully and as sensitively as she could. But I was fragile. I came from a broken and occasionally violent and uncertain home-life. My father was an alcoholic. And because of that I was someone who worked more from instinct than intellect. An asset. And a liability.

Ironically it was this trait - this instinct - that finally cost me dear. If not her love, then her companionship. And her friendship. Instinct was trumped and then trampled by fear. The fear and fright of losing her. Like a ship-wrecked sailor desperately holding on to any flotsam, I did the same. I didn't want to lose her. She was everything to me. I panicked. And in so doing, I lost her forever.

The wisdom of the years. Oh to have been cool. And measured. And to have played the long game. But I was young. I was madly in love. And when caught up in the madness of love even the wisest of men act irrationally – philosophers and poets - writers and painters too, many of whom, who over the centuries have acted similarly. The madness of summer love. So why should young Retep have been any different?

My Life Closed Twice Before Its Close

My life closed twice before its close—
It yet remains to see
If Immortality unveil
A third event to me

So huge so hopeless to conceive
As those that twice befell.
Parting is all we know of heaven.
And all we need of hell.

Emily Dickinson

Alison was the first of the three great loves that I've been lucky enough to have had. Ruth followed. A story for another day. I thereafter met my wife. An Alison too. But as the first, so she remains forever more - the first.

When you're young and vital and sensory alive to the world and its new experiences she and those days are not something you forget easily. Or wish to. Well, at the end of the affair that's all you want to do. To forget. To have some peace and tranquillity. A release from the pain. And the torture, physical as well as emotional, from which you're suffering. You're rocked. And knocked for six. You're left reeling and spinning. But conversely you don't want to forget either. Well, how could you. Do you really wish to erase and eradicate the immediate past? All that you lived for. And developed a life together only to wipe away that season in the sun? Of course the answer is no. It wasn't part of my nature or my psyche to do so. And if I'd moved on easily it would have been shallow not reflecting what our relationship meant to me. Instead, what you really you want is it all back again. Like a child. You want someone to make it all better again. Your heart's desire. Like Oliver Twist with his bowl and spoon pleading - can I please have some more sir?

And whilst I can't be certain because there are gaps in my 1976 diary I don't think she was thereafter in touch or enquired as to my welfare. Unless it was from afar. And unknowing to me.

Instead, and appropriately, after Christmas, it was cold turkey.

With no lifts from Meadowbank to Dunfermline College; with the demands of academia and perhaps her reaching the conclusion to ease away from the sport, our paths thereafter rarely crossed.

But of course life went on. After all the only alternative is for it to end.

And so the days passed. At times painfully. Slowly. And then of a sudden you arrive in a bright new land. A new place. And before you realise it the years and the decades have rushed by too. When your plans and dreams got in the way of living.

But in writing of our love story I still feel for that young man. His heady joys. His deep despair.

Later, I saw things more clearly. From a distance I can see how tactically naive Retep was with his impulsive mistakes. You so wish to place a fatherly arm around him. And say 'No! No! No! Don't do that. Do this instead!'

But when you're in love you're not normal. And perhaps what makes us so attractive to others is the way we act. Even if it is impulsively. Particularly in matters of the heart.

But today I would advise - don't pester her at 8:30 in the morning – don't send her that bunch of flowers when she wants time apart – give her time and space – let things ebb and flow - allow your world and her's to find its natural balance and space. Don't phone her for a while. Give her time to miss you rather than drown her with unwanted attention. Wait for the moment. It might yet come.

Alison occasionally still appears in my dreams. She remains in a deep corner of my heart. And more so since I began writing this small memoir. But back then she was in Retep's thoughts. All the day long. And in his dreams through the night. And she will remain in my heart until my last breath. And that will be the end of our short but deeply felt love affair.

She is forever located in that first and best summer of my life. The summer of '75. Rooted in the timeless late summer evenings of Edinburgh. Under gentle zephyr breezes. Where still I locate her. And see her. And us. Two young inexperienced lovers. Walking around the former Meadowbank stadium. Or come the early autumn evenings which in Edinburgh were usually wet 'n windy and me driving her back in the snugness of my grandfather's car to her college room. To her alma mater.

Like the former Meadowbank Stadium, Dunfermline College of P.E. has suffered a similar fate falling to giant bull-dozers. But those two twin pillars of our past, still they remain and exist in my mind's eye. And in writing this brief memoir of our short love affair perhaps it will continue to so exist. As Shakespeare wrote, I give life to thee.

Much of our capital is still intact and still remains. And the associated memories of us travelling through the streets of the capital city. Driving slowly to contain the moment. Not wanting the young lovers' evening to draw to a conclusion. And a closure. Played out each time we were in the car together. How can I hold the moment and keep time's winged chariot at bay? As Springsteen sang 'I swear I'll drive all night.'

We savoured the moments. We drove sitting next to each other within the close contained intimate space that having the use of a car so wonderfully provides to lovers throughout the world. As it has done from the 1950s onwards. And probably continues so today.

When I took her home we drove through the Queen's Park. The countryside in the town. The Highlands in the city, with its small lochs and little mountain, Arthurs Seat. And then on past the fine old houses of Grange dappled in the evening's fading rays as the sun set in the west. And then past the middle class grey tenements of Morningside. And out to the airy south of the city. Where her architect father and lovely mother lived at Buckstone and Braid.

But before then we climbed up Comiston or Braid Road. And then down into the small dip and small valley of Hermitage. And the adjacent woodland estate of Braid. By the gently flowing, bubbling plashing stream of the Braidburn. And it was there we parked the car at the foot of the steep climb. Just past the bridge. And the entrance gate to the park. And the entrance to my heart.

The unresolvable question. How do I hold back time to savour the anticipation of those joyous and special moments that might come when we stopped the car for perhaps an hour if we were lucky. Those loving moments that young people wait years for and make life's apprenticeship worth serving. The colour amongst the grey. When we could begin to gently explore and enact out our dreams of what life could and might yet be. And all the while living in the moment. Believing such moments would endlessly repeat themselves. Like Groundhog Day. For ever more. And that our youth would be forever. And that how we feel this night – our passion - is how we would always feel for each other.

One can never truly capture and describe such elusive moments. They disappeared in the setting of the sun. And the rising of the moon above the hillside. But still I remember how that young lover felt.

And whilst Retep didn't have the capacity to put down in words how he felt I'm impressed that he writes an entry in his diary each day.

There's a part of him that wants to preserve the moment.

To record it so that it isn't lost for ever.

Only he doesn't quite know why or for what purpose.

He simply writes.

One journal begins in January. And closes in December.

And so it goes until today there are fifty such journals.

And so it goes on until one day there will be a last and a final entry.

And then no more.

Millions of words.

But to what purpose?

To say, look I was here? I lived a life. I don't want to be forgotten.

Or perhaps, all along it was for this very moment. The Way We Were.

Outside the Hermitage of Braid we'd sit and we'd talk into the evening.

In my shyness sometimes I might take a leap of faith and gently kiss her sweet inviting lips. And if I were brave there might be the tentative low rustling of clothing as we virginally and sweetly explored what love was enjoying its wondrous novelty and pleasures. We embraced. We kissed. I explored the softness and sweet mystery of her body. The refreshing joy of her mind. The vitality of her personality. Her youthful joie de vivre. She was on the cusp. The very early stage of moving toward her Edinburgh prime.

Sometimes we'd have to swiftly stop and look respectable when a solitary and very occasional dog-walker emerged from the Hermitage and walked by. We'd laugh and giggle.

Today, I'm older than those dog-walkers that we laughed at long ago.

But of course it broke the spell and what we'd been working towards all evening bringing such sweet moments to an abrupt end. But if our hopes had been dashed, still there would be other evenings and we were always mindful that the clock was slowly ticking. She of course was far more sensible than me. I'd have happily remained in her arms until the clock chimed midnight. But time's winged chariot called. And I couldn't stop the clock. She'd say, Peter, we better get up the road in case my parents are worried'. I'd say, 'Okay, just another five minutes.' And then there might be one further five minutes. But I was ever mindful of getting her home at a reasonable hour. And thus another exquisite day and evening would be brought to a closure.

But there remained one final pleasure.

As I drove home in the quietness of the late Edinburgh evening in what RLS called a dwam – a dream - I blissfully replayed our evening and our time together, playing it over and over all the way back home from the hills of Braid to the sea and to Portobello. Every conversation and each exchange minutely going over them in detail. My witticisms when I'd made her laugh or giggle. My faux pas' which made me squirm. And of the moments when we walked hand in hand or with my arm around her shoulders as the evening coolness gradually descended.

It's only from the view in winter that you consider some of the innumerable variables and imponderables at play. If Meadowbank hadn't existed. If we both hadn't enjoyed athletics. If I'd not had access to a car. And so it goes on.

From 1971 aged fourteen I began to keep a diary each day.

The first two were Letts Schoolboy Diaries.

For five years straight. 1971 through to the end of 1975. And the end of the affair in late 1975 aged nineteen years of age. I was assiduous with daily entries never missing a day. And then come the beginning of a New Year - January 1976 - the diaries stutter and lapse into intermittent entries for the rest of the year. The only occasion I would do so for the whole decade of the 1970s.

Was it because I remained in shock?

Was it because we'd parted and I knew life might never be quite the same again?

But a line had been drawn in the sand.

That fragile and reflective boy had begun to garner and learn some of the harsh lessons and truths of life.

That it doesn't always end well.

There's not always a Clarence. A guardian angel to look after my well-being and my best interests. At best he had gone off duty or moved elsewhere. More probably he had never existed.

There was no Magwitch looking after my best interests from afar.

I was alone.

And I was lonely.

I'd awoken not just to a New Year but to a new dawn. A new life without the person I loved the most. Did I really want to write about life without her in my world? The world had become a harder place to live in and inhabit and I realised it would forever more hold such tough experiences.

The young boy would have to become a man. Or at least strive to do so as best as he could.

The days of 1976 became weeks.

The weeks became months.

And before I knew it the months had become years.

1975 became 1985. A decade since we parted.

1985 became 1995. The following year, 1996, I moved to the Highlands.

And now it's forty five years later.

And if it's not night, then it's dusk.

And here I am in the early winter of life reflecting upon the McCartney song 'Will you still love me, when I'm 64?'

To my knowledge I haven't spoken to Alison in all the years since the end of 1978.

But on one occasion our paths accidentally crossed. Like ships in the night. But in the light.

I was on a return visit to Edinburgh.

She was walking into The Gyle shopping precinct.

As I rounded a bend toward the exit, a blonde vision of loveliness dashed past me pushing what looked like twin boys in a push chair.

Should I seek her out?

She too could have turned around. And spoken to me.

But she didn't.

Which in its way said something.

Perhaps everything.

And before we knew it the moment had passed.

My instinct had failed me. Again.

As well as my courage.

I needed to get back to the car.

But did I?

She was in a hurry.

A momentary blink of an eye.

But she'd reacted.

For just a giveaway second.

That she too had recognised me.

Perhaps there's a metaphor there.

The 1976 diary makes less than a handful of references to her.

But there is one appearance which surprised me. I didn't think I'd ever visited her home high up above the city on the hills of Braid at Buckstone. I only ever dropped her on her doorstep. But I may be wrong on that account and instead visited her just the once come the early autumn in late September of 1976 when I was supposed to be going off south to study at Loughborough University (but that's another story). I record that I've dropped by to visit her with some flowers noting that she was depressed, which wasn't like her at all.

The second but last entry records how on my return from the Montreal Olympics I'd taken her out for her birthday.

Was that THE lost opportunity?

I was a year older.

And a little wiser.

Throughout the evening she had been tender and loving toward me. It was as if nothing had changed. It had remained 1975. And that everything since had just been a bad dream. A nightmare.

Could I have resurrected the past?

And brought her back into my life.

After all she remained deep in my heart.

The poignant crossroads of life.

The roads not travelled.

The opportunities lost and forever gone.

The land of lost content.

If only they'd been better signposted. What then?

But the moment passed me by.

But what might have happened if I'd tried to woo her one last time? Perhaps I'd developed an indifferent sensibility. The previous month I'd met Ruth. Was there a new small maturity and sensibility not to have pursued her? But looking back. Perhaps that was actually the occasion to have been impetuous.

A life not led.

A parallel universe.

Or would we still have remained incompatible?

Only the gods might know.

They say that one partner loves the other more.

Would that have been our fate?

One loving.

And the other only liking?

Regrettably the diaries of 1975 are not what they became three years later in 1978 when they become full to overflowing.

What good diaries should be. Not only does '78 detail actions and facts and the what and the wherefore, but conversations too. Boswell like. But importantly also my reactions. My responses. My opinions as to what happened and to what people did or said. The best diaries are of course gossipy. And opinionated. And indiscreet.

Thus the 1975 diary - The Way We Were - contains mainly short notes or passages briefly recording some of my feelings.

But still.

The thread is there.

The story is there.

And the journey from optimistic beginning to bitter conclusion is there too.

And the hard and miserable winter that signalled the end of the affair.

That December 1975 evening remains forever etched in my mind.

Our parting words.

My tears as I drove across the darkness of the capital from Cramond, past Inverleith Park and on to Meadowbank seeing the city through the prism of tear-stained eyes whilst outside the car window the world was oblivious and unaware and unconcerned about my plight.

My sadness.

My loneliness.

Two had become one.

Under the sulphurous Edinburgh street lights of the city her citizens passed by huddled up in heavy coats bent into the wet and the wind silhouetted against the dark night sky.

And the bitter cold. And the damp of early winter.

That oh so familiar happy journey from Meadowbank to her college rooms, this was now the last such journey.

So this was how it ended.

This is how death feels.

How could that be?

It was a time of firsts.

It was a time of lasts.

And the conversations and the lovers' talk of our youth. They simply disappeared into the ether, vanishing in the gale that had engulfed me.

To that great place in the sky where all such lovers' conversations go.

I don't even have a photograph of the two of us together.

Others may have such a thing, but not me.

All I have is an old newspaper cutting from a July edition of a 1973 East Lothian Courier of the two of us sitting together on a tartan blanket at the Musselburgh Highland Games. And even there she remains tantalisingly elusive.

Half in and half out of the photograph.

Already beginning the slow act of presciently disappearing from my life.

I revisit the city of my youth and drive past old haunts in the bright summer light or in the pale sky of winter. Perhaps appropriately neither Dunfermline College of P.E. her alma mater nor Meadowbank our alma mater remain. But whilst we live, memories. Still they remain.

Only a few times in life are the stars perfectly aligned.

On one such occasion - it was a winter's Friday evening in her college room at Cramond. We were enveloped in each other's arms. Face to face. That was the time we should have become as one. It's heart-breaking to recall that evening now. And that lost opportunity which never arose again.

And never will.

We'd spent that evening in complete harmony.

Memories.

But of course much of our city remains.

Morningside. Seeing her walking by on sun-kissed mornings. She in her school uniform going for a bus to take her out to Mary Erskine's School or coming home at dusk, whilst I was making my downcast way to and from work, employed in the job of a lowly cost clerk whilst she was vital and vivacious and sunny and full of life about the lovely progress she was making in the world.

There was Binns' Corner. Where we sometimes met under the stars. As well as the old clock.

Similar to James Salter 'I imagined too the places she walked in her girlhood, in her youth and in her perfection, long ago.'

I see her still after school walking along Princes Street with a boy. As my bus passed them my heart leaped up into my throat.

Oh, to have been able to swap places with that lucky guy.

How wonderful life would be.

In another book, 'A Life in A Day in a Year' she has a starring role appearing anonymously under the pseudonym Pixie Mia Farrow lookalike.

Within the book's introduction I write of how '...from a distance of forty years I can now discern patterns and key mistakes which of course tear at the soul and clutch at the heart.

They say 'if' is the saddest word in the English language.

If only I'd played a smarter, less intemperate and more measured hand with the lovely Pixie (Alison) or as rather beautifully expressed by Father Gianni in the BBC series set in Tuscany, 'Second Chance Summer' '...the problem is you only learn with age and experience so by the time you realise you have learnt a lot of things, unfortunately a lot of time has passed and many chances have been lost.'

I go on to write 'But if I were to be offered some Faustian pact whereby I could travel back in time and change some key staging posts in life, tempting as it might be to accept, I'd probably reject the Devil's offer preferring the way life worked out afterwards, but of course, shades of the film 'Sliding Doors' spring to mind.

And having revisited these journals after four decades and lived with them over recent months, as I drift off to sleep of a summer's evening (now, upon a winter's night), ethereal dreams and visions of Pixie (Alison) still occasionally dance across the screen and the night air and haunting images of crossroads in life not taken, offer tantalising glimpses of a different life not led with all their interesting unexplored avenues.'

1972

Age 16

Thursday 28th September 1972 An 8.00 a.m. start at Thomas Graham & Sons Ltd. Builders & Plumbers Merchants so that means getting the 7.30 a.m. 16 bus from Oxgangs down to Morningside. I suppose it's easier than getting the 6.00 a.m. bus when I did my paper round at Baird's Newsagent's Morningside Drive. I can report work is still quite exciting as I walk along to it. Our boss Roy Wallace started Scott and me doing some pricing of the invoices. Just basic stuff. We take ages to do it as we have to look up big volumes to find the price of each item. Roy's like one of these computers you see on 'Tomorrow's World'. He's got it all stored in his big brain and just whizzes through it. At lunchtime Scott and I went along to Morningside again for our lunch. I'm beginning to like him more and more. He's a nice guy. In the afternoon I was allowed to use the phone. I called my sister Anne who's down at Nana's at Porty. Back home I had my tea. I then went down to Meadowbank. ~~ILLEGIBLE~~ in money. Apart from the running, half the fun is all the girls there. Despite me having a second rate job and her attending posh Mary Erskine's I may be able to get a date with the lovely Alison. She's good fun. We seem to hit it off.

Tuesday 3rd October 1972. Thomas Graham's was much better today. I actually quite enjoyed it which was a bit of a relief after yesterday. Perhaps it was just because it was a Monday. I did more pricing. My boss Roy is a pretty funny bloke. We had a few laughs. I went for a walk up to Morningside Park and sat out in the sunshine for a bit. Once again it was great to be able to go down to Meadowbank in the evening. I've decided that I'm taking up the 800 metres.

I'm keen to train regularly. On the girls front there are three in my life just now. I'm pretty pally with 'Ginger'; Alison; and Anne Sowersby. I managed to get a lift home to Oxgangs. It makes an enormous difference getting in just after nine o'clock.

Thursday 12th October 1972 Thomas Graham & Son's wasn't quite so bad although I'm not sure what happened to Scott Wallace. He didn't come back in in the afternoon after his haircut – most odd. He's been off quite a few times now given this is only our third week. I wonder if he's regretting leaving school too. I went straight down to Meadowbank on the 15 bus. As it wound its way along Princes Street I spotted Alison in her Mary Erskine uniform walking along with Ronnie. My heart took a start. I thought how great it would be to get off with her. I got back to Oxgangs in time to watch a wee bit telly.

Monday 13th November 1972 It was a queer sort of day at work but I couldn't quite put my finger on why. It was a cold parky day. I enjoyed being out at lunchtime - quite refreshing. Perhaps one of the reasons why it was odd being at work was that I hadn't thought about it once over the weekend because I'd really enjoyed myself. I'm really glad to have gone back to athletics. It means Paul and I will keep up with each other. In the evening I went to Meadowbank. Mr Walker gave us the toughest and hardest session ever. It was 8 x 400 metres. That gave me something to think about. And it soon warmed us up too. Anyway I managed to do it but I'm a bit of a wimp. Keeping my options open I fancy two classy girls - Anne (was it Sowersby or Johnstone?) and Alison. Oh. I meant to say my new training shoes arrived from Mum's Chorlton Catalogue. They're Hunt - red and white. They're different from everybody else which I'm quite pleased about. They're quite stylish. I'm really pleased with them. I got home quite late. I'm now off to bed. Good Night Retep.

Thursday 14ᵗʰ December 1972 - Remember To Get A New Diary Work is going along quite nicely just now. I think it's with Christmas on the horizon. After tea I went up to Meadowbank. The training wasn't quite so hard tonight. I was able to take it in my stride which was good allowing me to show off a bit. Alison and her pal - what's her name – Wendy Boxer - I think are both nice looking. When I got home it was very enjoyable snuggling up by the remains of the fire watching Colditz. I really enjoy it. Bernard Hepton is so good as the Kommandant - feeling for Colonel Preston's dire news about the death of his wife but knowing he can't cross the line in their twin roles. It's consistently good. I've just gone to bed now. Disappointingly my radio doesn't sound too good, with poor reception.

1973

Tuesday 20ᵗʰ February 1973 On the way out to Morningside Gaga's car was jerking quite badly. I hope for his sake that it's okay. He never has much luck with his cars. I always feel sorry for him. It would be nice to be well off and to be able to buy him a decent car. I'm back on top of the podium again after winning lunchtime's game of 'Scrabble'. A bit of a first at work - the day passed very quickly mainly because I was enjoying the type of tasks that I was given to do. It stretched me slightly more than the usual mundane stuff. Late afternoon Roy gave me a lift along Morningside to pick up his Edinburgh Evening News. He partly gets it for the details of the greyhound racing at Wallyford. I went training this evening. I was running fantastically well; so much so I got three new personal bests. Alison was along. She's lovely. I quite like her. I think Anne

Sowersby fancies me. I came home to enjoy my favourite tea - Nana's macaroni.

Thursday 22nd February 1973 Gaga gave me another run straight to Graham's front door saving me from a long walk along Balcarres Street carrying my training kit. As ever very good of him and much appreciated. He looks after me well. It was a bit of a slow morning. In the afternoon I rang Nana twice. And then Paul. I am going to Meadowbank early this evening. We got our pay this afternoon - a day early. It'll encourage the skivers to take tomorrow off! I went training. A rubbish session. I really fancy Anne Johnstone. Paul and I were playing against her, Alison and Evelyn at basketball - great fun. I came home and had a late dinner. I'm now about to dive off to bed.

Saturday 5th May 1973 I was up early to get the E.A.C. bus through to Pitreavie. The bus driver was late. I thought Alison ran well to finish second. Both Rangers and Sunderland won their respective Scottish and English Cups with the latter's victory a nice surprise against Leeds who were massive favourites. In the evening I sat in watching the telly. An excellent night's viewing with Planet of the Daleks (Dr Who); an Elvis film Flaming Star; Dick Emery; Ironside and then Sportsreel. I've got a terrible cold which is a pity given I'm making my 400 metres debut tomorrow in the Young Athletes League. It's my first ever proper race over the quarter mile.

Tuesday 22nd May 1973 It was pouring with rain this morning. However the day passed quite quickly. I gave Mum a tinkle at her Civil Service work. Late afternoon I nipped along to Morningside for an Edinburgh Evening News for Roy. In return he's going to give me some overtime. Gaga gave me a lift up to training. Mandy

McLean was there this evening. I was speaking to Alison. When she's at Mary Erskine's tomorrow she's going to let Moira Cameron know I was asking for a date. Stuart Gillies gave me a lift home.

Thursday 24th May 1973 A lovely start to the morning. I bumped into the lovely Alison at Morningside. She was on her way in to Mary Erskine School. I briefly spoke to her. Marion forgot to bring me in my tape recorder so that was a bit of a disappointment. The morning was a bit of a bore. Roy ran Pat Haldane and Gillian home and then took me for some chips. I went training. I was running quite well except my knee is hurting a bit. Mandy McLean is a bit of an OOOH! Not that she would look at me. I got home quite late on.

Monday 28th May 1973 On my way to pick up my Hornet comic from Bairds at Morningside Drive I saw Alison on her way to Mary Erskine School. My heart soars whenever I see her. Is it possible to get a lovelier start to the working week? That's a rhetorical question. The work day flew by. At the end of play I was quite lucky getting a lift home all the way from Morningside to Portobello from old Jimmy Wilson. Although he has a quick temper Jimmy's a classy wee fellow. He's a very dapper dresser and friendly with a wee bit of class. For years you can understand why he was Graham & Sons representative. He's got a neat little Triumph Herald. It goes with his image. The car is a replacement for the Ford Cortina company car he used to have. He's done better in life than Grandpa Willie. He owns his own house; has a better car; and earns his corn in an easier way too. Since he's retired he's now working beside us part-time in the Costing Department. His health is much better than Will's too. In the evening Gaga gave me a lift out to Saughton to run in the Scottish Young Athletes' League. I won the 200 metres in a not bad time. Later Eric Fisher was very good giving me a lift all the way home via Coach Walker's house where we dropped by for a chat.

Monday 11th June 1973 I went along to work early this morning. I played football out in the yard at lunchtime. I was meant to be competing down at Longniddry this evening. However Roy didn't let me away early. We ended up waiting on a bus down the east coast. In the end Arthur Groundwater picked us up and drove us down there. I ran rubbishly. We came back to Meadowbank. Back in the cafeteria I was talking with the lovely Alison. I didn't get to bed until eleven o'clock.

Tuesday 12th June 1973 Last evening after racing at Longniddry I enjoyed speaking with Alison in the Meadowbank cafeteria. This morning on my way in to work I saw her at Morningside on her way to Mary Erskine's School. My cup runneth over...

Age 17

Sunday 15th July 1973 I was back into Graham's this morning to work some further overtime. That's quite unusual but I was relatively happy to do so as it was pretty straightforward heading down to Morningside from Oxgangs. Come lunchtime I headed out to Musselburgh to take part in their annual Highland Games. I got a second in the 100 metres and also a third in the 400 metres. I spent some of the time sitting with the lovely Alison. Afterwards a group of us wandered down to Luca's to get some of their delicious ice cream before making the long way back to Oxgangs. It would have been easier going back to Porty at the end of the day but I guess you can't have it both ways. Les Ramage is going to come over at ten o'clock.

The author and Alison at the 1973 Musselburgh Highland Games

Wednesday 5th September 1973 As I was pricing plumbing invoices work passed quite quickly today. Roy had a wee dig at me as is his way from time to time. He told me 'You're not a Cost Clerk - instead you're a Junior Cost Clerk.' If it wasn't so sad you'd have to laugh. Come teatime Scott Wallace and I accompanied each other to Rankin Drive before I headed down to get the 42 bus at the King's Buildings. Gaga gave me a lift up to Meadowbank. Anne and Iain were down so they were in the car too. It was a really tough session tonight as I joined the middle distance group. Alison is not bad looking. I'd like to bag off with her on Saturday at the dance after this weekend's Europa Cup. Scott Brodie gave me a lift home.

Sunday 9th September 1973 I got up at half past eight. I did a training session. It was a bleak cold and wet afternoon but the Europa Cup was good. Great Britain had some victories. It really got the big crowd going including Chris

Monk in the 200 metres; Andy Carter in the 800 and Brendan Foster in the 5000 metres. It was really enjoyable stuff. I really fancy Alison or Fiona Macaulay. Iain is staying with us tonight. The two of us enjoyed lying back watching Carry on Constable having a good laugh. It was just like old times at Oxgangs.

Monday 10th September 1973 After dropping Iain back at Oxgangs so that he could go in to Firrhill School it was down to Thomas Graham's to work. Gaga dropped me off at the door of 51 Balcarres Street. It must be close to my first anniversary here at 'Dickensville'. However the day passed quite quickly as I had my Athletics Weekly but mainly because I spent all of today day-dreaming about Alison. I was back home by 5.45 p.m. before going out to run a very hard session with the middle distance runners. I was 'out the box' for about ten minutes afterwards. Someone must have upset Alison. I noticed she was crying. I was greeting too but for other reasons - 600s by way of example! Later we played cards together. We're travelling through to Grangemouth by train on Saturday. I wonder if I'll be able to sum up the courage to suggest a game of mixed doubles at tennis next Monday on the Edinburgh Holiday. I think that would be a good time to ask her.

Tuesday 11th September 1973 Before making my way along Balcarres Street I sat in Gaga's car reading his Scottish Daily Express. Muhammed Ali beat Ken Norton on points. There was a nip in the air. And a light frost about. I like these kind of mornings. Everything is fresh with a whole new day ahead of me. It's just a shame I have to spend most of it cooped up inside Thomas Graham & Sons. However it wasn't too bad. Nana gave me a wee ring. I looked in to see Mum briefly before going out to

Roy's house at Lasswade for lunch. His wife is pregnant. Later I phoned Paul. In the evening. Alison got on my wick calling me by my last name 'Hoffmann'. Scott ran Duncan, Dougie and me home. Top Thirty tonight.

Wednesday 12th September 1973 It was quite nippy again this morning. I sat in the car and read the paper. The morning passed quite quickly and so did part of the afternoon. Scott and I had to wait ages for the 41 bus at Morningside Drive so I was late in by the time I'd made my way down to the King's Buildings for a 42. Also I didn't get a lift up to Meadowbank from Gaga tonight so a disaster on the bus front today. Paul looks as if he is going to get off with Alison. It was a terrible sort of an evening. I watched the Paul Newman film. Good night Retep.

Friday 14th September 1973 Roy went home at ten o'clock this morning. His wife wasn't very well. I didn't have too much work to do today. We got away early at half past four. It didn't help me any as I had to wait a while in the car for Gaga to finish up at Waugh the Butcher's. I've decided to send for my driving licence. I stayed in and watched the telly – The Law and Jake Wade followed by It's A Knockout. Paul phoned up later. He's as good as bagged off with Alison – lucky boy!

Sunday 23rd September 1973 Gaga ran Anne home to Oxgangs and dropped me off at Meadowbank. We did quite a hard session. Paul doesn't want off with Alison anymore. Iain is staying with us tonight so that's quite good fun. We sat and watched a film together. I've come to the end of my Carlton Shorthand Notebook and first training diary so will need to get another one from Thomas Graham & Son Ltd and start a fresh one tomorrow.

Tuesday 25th September 1973 I took a flask of Nana's homemade soup into work today. That's the first time I've done that. It's to help economise a bit. I drove the car a bit. Willie Fernie phoned up Chapman's today on my behalf to ask about a Bond Bug. I've set my heart on getting one. I am seriously thinking about buying one. At lunchtime on his way back to Portobello Gaga dropped by outside Graham's and picked up the flask. I wished I was just heading back with him to Portobello for the afternoon instead of staying on at work. Scott phoned in to say he's not coming back to work until next Monday. That's a disappointment. After work I bumped into Chris Waite. He's a nice guy. I was running very well again this evening. I told Alison that Paul didn't want off with her any longer.

Thursday 27th December 1973 I didn't feel too good when I awoke this morning. I phoned Bill up. Iain got his new radio for Christmas. I travelled down to Waugh's Butcher shop at lunchtime to meet Gaga. In the afternoon we had our first day back at training. It was great to be able to train at this time rather than being stuck in at work. Later Paul and I beat Scott Brodie and the good badminton player Alan Bowes in a doubles take-on at table tennis. In the evening I stayed down and did some blockwork with Alison and her coach Stuart Gillies. I was talking with Fiona Macaulay. I'd like to get off with her. Stuart Gillies gave me a lift home afterwards – straight to the door – good lad!

Evening: Weights session; blockwork – terrible 32 metres times 4.3; 4.6; 4.4; 4.6 secs (Alison did 4.6 secs)

1974

Tuesday 22nd January 1974 It was quite a quick day at work today mainly because I was working really hard. The time just seemed to pass by rather easily. It was one of those days (rare) that you feel at one with your (working) environment – a good feeling. After work oh how my heart soared. I walked up to the foot of Morningside Drive to get the 41 bus. Alison was on her way home from Mary Erskine's School. She saw me and came across the road to talk to me. She's such a nice girl. I would love to go about with her. For once the bus came too soon. I thought about her for much of the journey home, but forlornly. Alison in her public school uniform, bubbling and sparkling with intelligence and prospects, while little old me is working as a lowly cost clerk at Tommy Graham's. I can but dream. As Yeats says:

He Wishes For The Clothes Of Heaven

'...But I, being poor, have only my dreams:
I have spread my dreams under your feet;
Tread softly because you tread on my dreams.'

W.B. Yeats

Sunday 27th January 1974 Nana, Heather and wee Anne were away with the Edinburgh Mineral Club to Montrose. I drove the car up to Meadowbank. Anne Johnstone and Alison were both squeezing up to me in the Meadowbank cafe. Afterwards Dougie let me drive his car home. In the afternoon I watched the Commonwealth Games highlights on the telly before driving Anne and Iain home to Oxgangs in the evening with Gaga in the car of course. We watched The Onedin Line. It was actually very good featuring the Great Garibaldi as a passenger under threat. It was the last episode in this series. Afterwards there was an interesting play on which featured the wrestler Adrian Street – a strange juxtaposition but very watchable. I wouldn't mind bagging off with Alison. I spend idle hours thinking of her. Will I ever take her out? I don't agree with Barrie! Hmmm, perhaps I do.

The Little Minister

"Let no one who loves be called altogether unhappy. Even love un-returned has its rainbow."

James Barrie

Sunday 10th February 1974 In the morning I drove the car up to Meadowbank. I wasn't running very well at all. I couldn't run very fast as my left hamstring was really niggling. However on a positive note I've got my starting blocks position and numbers off to a T. In the afternoon I watched a basketball match with Davie Reid. He's actually a nice guy but he doesn't half talk a lot. I could hardly get to watch the game. From now on I'm going to try to do mobility stretching every evening to see if it will help prevent me getting any more injuries. Also if I'm wanting to do well this season I better get the finger out and start to train really hard. I mean the last few weeks I've been slacking. So from now on I am going to work hard. Late afternoon Bill Walker gave Sandy Sutherland and me a lift home. Later on I drove Will's car out to Oxgangs. On the way I saw Alison at Morningside. How my heart soared. Or is that sored! Before bed I sat and watched a good film called Mrs Miniver. A classic of its type and really very touching indeed.

Thursday 14th February 1974 Although I sent a Valentine card to Alison I didn't receive one in return. I went up to Meadowbank at half past six with Gaga giving me a lift. It was snowing for about ten minutes. After training Paul and I went out with Dougie McLean and Scott Brodie to the Waverley Bar and then on to the St Valentine's college dance. It was really good. If I'd wanted to I could have got off with three girls. It finished at 2.30 a.m. I didn't get to bed until 3.30 a.m. I'll pay for it!

Tuesday 19th February 1974 Given it's still the middle of February it was quite a nice day out. And work was fine too. Both the morning and afternoon ticked along nicely. I phoned up an insurance company to ask for a quotation for insuring Dougie's car. It was quite reasonable. In the evening I ran a really good session starting to flow, running with power and rhythm. I think Alison knows that it was me who sent her the Valentine card. In fact touch wood the way things are going I could perhaps just get off with her. She says she may be going along to the disco after the Carnethy Hill Races at Penicuick on Saturday evening. I'm really hoping she will go along.

Thursday 21st February 1974 Apart from a slight zephyr it was a really nice day out today. The working day passed really very quickly. Indeed the whole week has. It's partly to do with looking forward to the prospect of Alison going along to Carnethy on Saturday evening. At lunchtime I played football out in the yard with the warehouse lads. I was kind of late after having my tea so Gaga allowed me to take the car up to Meadowbank. I ran a good training session. I was talking with Bill Walker afterwards for around ten minutes. He said I should be aiming to win the 1978 Commonwealth Games 800 metres gold medal! I saw Alison this evening but I wasn't talking to her. Wee Anne was down at Meadowbank again. I think she quite enjoyed herself. It was good to see her talking with one or two of the girls. Scott had his old boy's car along this evening – it's a powerful beast.

Saturday 23rd February 1974 Although it was a Saturday I went to work at Graham's all morning. Mark Wilson and

Paul arrived outside the showroom at 11.45 a.m. but we didn't manage to get a Penicuik bus until 12.40 p.m. I ran really well in the Youth's Carnethy Hill Race cross country getting the bronze medal with Paul winning it. The three of us had tea at Mr Scott's. When I heard that Alison was going to the disco, God! I could hardly disguise my excitement! Well, no wonder after all those years of holding a candle for her. The night went fabulously well. I got off with Alison. Even though the disco wasn't that good I just loved spending the whole evening in her company and most delicious of all we had a long kiss whilst we danced in each other's arms to The Hollies The Air That I Breathe. The evening was just fabulous. It went like a dream. I didn't really want it to end. I walked her down the road to where her dad was collecting her. I've never felt so happy in all my life. However that wasn't the end of the evening. Several of us got jumped by a large gang of local youths. I ended up getting my head kicked in. The police picked up two of the guys. Paul and I went round to Mr McCauley's house where we stayed the night. My head is really sore but I'm not really bothered as I'm sitting well above Cloud 9. I'm just so pleased to be off with the girl of my dreams. We stayed up until 1.45 a.m. before retiring to our beds. Quite a day. I don't think I'll ever forget it!

Sunday 24th February 1974 The day after the night before when I got off with Alison. After such an ethereal dream-like evening I could only come back down to planet Earth with a bang. It felt a funny sort of a day. Paul and I breakfasted with the McCauley family then phoned Mr Scott at 9.30 a.m. to get a lift in from Penicuik to Meadowbank. I wasn't talking with Alison for all that long. It was slightly awkward being back in the group situation. I didn't like to spend more time with her than anyone else. However we've arranged to go out together on Friday evening. I think the best way to stay off with her is to just sort of play it cool and not to try to monopolise her or anything like that.

Tuesday 26th February 1974 I got up at about nine o'clock. I spent the morning reading and listening to the radio. In the afternoon I drove the car out to Oxgangs. I popped in to Pentland Community Centre and then went down to 6/2 Oxgangs Avenue. I gave Mum her birthday present – 38 today. In the evening I ran quite a good session. Afterwards I was talking with Alison in the Meadowbank Café. We've arranged to meet on Friday at 6.30 p.m. It's our first official date!

Thursday 28th February 1974 With thinking about taking Alison out to the pictures tomorrow the day at Thomas Graham & Son's passed really quickly. At lunchtime I looked out to Oxgangs. I bumped into Mrs (Marion) Dibley and her younger daughter Lesley on the 16 bus. Only Iain was at home. Both Mum and John were in town together. I told Iain to let Mum know that after taking Alison to the pictures tomorrow that to expect me as I'll probably just stay there overnight. Because of the General Election there is no training this evening as Meadowbank is being prepared so as I was in no particular hurry to get home I just took the number 5 bus from Morningside Station to the top of Durham Road.

Friday 1st March 1974 Great stuff, I'll soon be going out with Alison. I was counting down the hours as the day went by. At lunchtime I went up to Oxgangs to see Mum and John. On the way, there was an amazing snow blizzard outside Graham's on Balcarres Street with the largest snowflakes I've ever seen. The flakes were massive. Gaga picked me up after work to allow me to get ready and then dropped me off so that I could meet Alison outside the pictures at half past six. By dint of nerves or just that I'm so thick I bought the wrong tickets and discovered as we were going in that the tickets were for Enter the Dragon. Well that was embarrassing. I had to go back to the kiosk to change the tickets for Paper Moon in front of everyone. The film wasn't very good. But we ended up having a smashing time. I took Alison home on the bus. We walked up the hill to Buckstone adjacent to the Braid Hills. On the way she said she can't go out very often as she has to study hard for her exams. What could I say to that - an unarguable position? A disappointing journey back home from the Braid Hills to Oxgangs where I was staying overnight; especially after all the keen anticipation and promise of the day.

Saturday 2nd March 1974 After staying at Oxgangs last night I took the 5 bus down to Porty this morning to collect my training bag. I then went straight up to Meadowbank to meet Bill's squad. The bus journey gave me lots of time to reflect on last evening's date with Alison to come to terms with the fact that she can't go out often because of her studying. We all travelled down to Gullane Beach to do a training session on the sand dunes. It was really fantastic. It was a very hard but very enjoyable group session. We ran about a mile and a half as a warm-up with Bill leading us out. We then did ten runs up a sand-dune with a jog back down recovery; then we did two hops up it on our left leg followed by our right leg and then bunny hops up it too. After a breather we ran a further mile on the sands and then had a competitive relay up and down more sand-dunes doing around five repetitions each which got us all breathing out our arses! We then ran a mile along the beach next to the Firth of Forth nice and relaxed. To finish off we had a race up and down the second last dune. I was first; Keith Ridley was second; and Paul was third. On that particular sand-dune I did three runs/staggers/walks! up it and jogged back down. By this time I was really shattered, but still going well; then on the last dune we did some 5 circuits. In the afternoon Drew Hislop drove Paul, Mark Wilson and me up town. We wandered about but I ended up not buying anything. In the evening I went out to Broomhouse Place to Paul's home for tea. In the evening we went out to see Enter the Dragon. We thought we'd never get in as the queue was so big. It went around the block. But somehow we did. The film was really fantastic!

Gullane Sands 2 hours training session

Sunday 3rd March 1974 At half past ten I wandered up to Meadowbank. I ran quite a good session especially given my legs must still have been feeling some of the effects of running on the sand-dunes yesterday. I also remained there all afternoon too. I was feeling a bit sorry for myself and felt a bit depressed about not being able to go about with Alison. I'd built my hopes up. I guess I'll just have to get her out of my mind. I can tell that Anne Sowersby and Petrina Cox both want off with me. The latter gave me a loan of her Jim Ryun book. She'd loaned me the Peter Snell book last week. There's a good sad film on the TV this evening. No doubt I'll be thinking of Alison when it's on.

Monday 4th March 1974 Oh no, Monday again! Actually the day passed quite quickly and wasn't too bad. At lunchtime I joined a few others and went out for a Chinese three course lunch special at the Mei Kwei Restaurant. In the evening I ran quite a good session. I decided to run the whole way in lane 3 with the group inside me to make me work harder. I felt quite tired after it but pleased. I'm going to do at least a mile warm down every evening. I'm feeling in pretty good shape. I'm looking forward to competing in the British Junior Indoor Championships for the first time later this month as a first year athlete. I smiled at and spoke once to Alison. I think that I'm already beginning to forget her. Once home I watched Colditz – my main TV staple.

Once again it was very good. It was all about an American mole in the camp. There was a very clever and surprise answer.

I Do Not Love Thee

'...I know I do not love thee! yet alas!
Others will scarcely trust my candid heart:
And oft I catch them smiling as they pass
Because they see me gazing where though art.'

Lady Caroline Norton

Friday 8th March 1974 It was an average sort of workday. Whilst at work I telephoned the Midland Counties AAAs at lunchtime. Thank goodness I'm entered for my first British Junior Indoor Championships. From there I popped up to Oxgangs. Last night I dreamt of Alison. I thought I'd got her out of my mind, but no. I think it was probably all the references to Mary Rand's daughter, Alison, in her autobiography that triggered it. Plus Rand looks like Alison too. But all today at work I've been thinking about her. At teatime Gaga picked me up outside the office. In the evening I went up to Meadowbank to do my weights session. Usually I'm the only athlete there on a Friday evening, so I got a pleasant surprise to see that athletics coach Stuart Gillies was there and guess who else? Yes, Alison! But I only managed to speak to her very briefly. All evening I've been thinking about her adding to my general miserableness and dissonance. Once back home I felt rather lonely.

Sunday 10th March 1974 I got up early. I took the car up to Meadowbank. I enjoyed a good game of squash with Davie Reid. Outside the weather is foul. I was talking with Alison for a bit. I wish I could forget about her especially as there are others who stand a much better chance of getting off with her than me. Ce la vie. I was asking John Anderson about this year's Easter course. In the evening I got in more driving practice as Gaga let me give Iain a lift home to Oxgangs. Come the evening there was a good film on called Lost Command – really excellent – leadership; betrayal; liberation – first class and very watchable. However, I wish I could get Alison out of my mind. I envy others who have a much better chance than me in the love stakes.

Saturday 18th May 1974 Paul and I got up around 9.30 a.m. Stewart Walters phoned up to say that he had got his scholarship pass from Edinburgh Corporation but had received no grant monies. When I heard Stewart's news I phoned up Nana. There was a letter for me too – yes! Nana opened it. She said I was the same. I've got a year's scholarship to get in to Meadowbank free but no money. A wee bit disappointing. It would have helped pay for my new spikes and allowed me to get a second pair too. Paul and I spent the morning in town just tootling around before heading down to Meadowbank Café to get a bite to eat. We were talking away with Alison, Derek Smith and Norman Gregor. Paul's asked Lorraine Morris out. She said she's already going about with someone else. A quiet evening in. It was unlike me to watch television but it was rather good this evening – Dr Who; a film Bandido about a Mexican revolutionary; Mike Yarwood and Cannon. All aided by a St Andrew's fish supper. And the additional enjoyment of a good Scotland team beating England 2-0.

Age 18

Monday 15th July 1974 Paul started work today at Thomas Graham & Sons whereas I'm getting my books in two weeks' time so there'll only be a short period of Forbes 'n

Hoffmann havoc at the 'blacking factory'. I wonder what kind of books they give you.

It poured with rain all day. I'm unsure what kind of sign that is from the gods. I'm pleased for Paul sake that he's got his first job and that I've been able to help him get the post. He's working upstairs in Ian Slater's department. Meanwhile I'm also pleased but to be getting out and escaping over the wall moving on to start on a new path in life.

Next month I'm going back to study at Telford College. I'm taking a couple of Highers and O levels. But this time unlike school I'm very motivated. I know I can do it. These are two major differences. For some reason I no longer doubt myself. I'm brighter than I've given myself credit for. And I know I'll apply myself and work assiduously. I think that's the big lesson that athletics has taught me since I began working at Graham's in September 1972.

Going on to win the Scottish Youth and then Junior titles has made me realise you only get back what you put in.

Since leaving Boroughmuir two years ago and starting working at Graham's has proven to be a pretty harsh lesson in life. At times it's been quite dispiriting. The nature of the work was not for me. And there were no prospects either. After only a few weeks in post I realised what a ghastly mistake I'd made. I came to regret skiving school for half the time leaving Boroughmuir with solitary O Levels in Arithmetic and History.

It's been soul-destroying coming in at 8.00 am. each day. I was cooped up inside in a window-less office with nine hours in front of me each day with no real autonomy.
And whilst sometimes seeing Alison either heading off to Mary Erskine School in the morning or occasionally

returning in the evening on her way home always raised my spirits it was also a kick in the teeth. It reinforced the contrast in our lives. She's bright and vivacious and out there doing something very positive with her life whilst for all intents and purposes I was like the young Charles Dickens over a century before at a similar age with no prospects in life heading back and forth each day to and from the blacking factory. It was like the 20th century meeting the 19th century.

I've never said how miserable I've been here always putting on a brave face to Mum and others. Even in agreeing a way forward with her support I've sold it or spun it that it's for positive reasons. However the reality is that I'd quickly mastered pricing interminable invoices within a few weeks. It wasn't stretching me at all.

Ultimately it's only been my athletics that has assuaged life here.

Of course it's not been entirely bad. I've grown up a bit. I've matured and am slightly more world-wisely. I like many of the people here particularly Willie Fernie. I'll miss our wee lunchtime games of chess. I've also enjoyed the wee social outings to the Silver Bowl Chinese Restaurant at Comiston Road for the three-course specials. And also to the International Restaurant. I've become good pals with Scott Wallace but he's left now too to better his life.

Along the way there have been many laughs. Roy's a funny and witty guy. I've had some tremendous laughs with him. It's hard to pick out the best amongst them. But I won't forget my first week. I'd paid a visit to the gents' loo. I was sitting quite contently in cubicle number one contemplating life, as one does on the shitter. Of a sudden from the cubicle next to me (cubicle number two) I heard someone groan out.

Eh what's that about? Then a foot appeared under the adjacent wall into my cubicle. What the fuck! I didn't say anything. I held my breath. What the fuck was going on here. It went silent for a minute. A deathly hush. I held my breath. Ten it started again. A ghostly shriek. Then a further groan. The foot became a shin. I held my breath. I was completely mesmerised. I stared intently down at this trousered leg only an inch or two from my own foot, so much so I was forgetting to breathe. Christ did that mean the guy's opposite leg was intruding in to cubicle number three? Was he completely splayed out? I was so mesmerised I couldn't move. The tension became unbearable. What would happen next? Of a sudden the intense silence was broken by a FUCKING LOUD cry followed by the most God Almighty enormous long-drawn out groan. And a further groan of intense pain. The next thing I knew the whole fucking leg appeared on top of my foot. I hopped off the lavy seat with my breeks half-way down my legs. Christ! I thought, that poor guy's got some constipation. I was going to shout through to enquire if he was all right but decided no. Instead I couldn't get my arse wiped quickly enough before scarpering back through to the office.

Fuck me what kind of a house of horrors had an innocent young sixteen year old landed up in! I sat down with beads of sweat running down my pow to try to focus on my work. A few minutes later Roy walks in to the room, rubs his hands and announces to one and all, with a wee wink in my direction and a scratch of his arse 'Ah that feels much better!' My introduction to the inimitable Roy Wallace.

But no, overall I've generally hated it here.

Balcarres Street has been a miserable wind tunnel, particularly when summer turned to autumn. Come the winter whilst it's been nice to get in to the warmth of the office one thereafter emerged out in to the darkness and cold at five o'clock.

Neither will I miss the long travail across town dashing up through Morningside Graveyard to get the 41 bus. But I will miss the wee bar of Needler's chocolate orange that I treated myself to from Guthrie's Morningside Drive to sustain me en-route home.

Neither will I miss running up Blackford Avenue and down West Mains Road to catch the 42 bus at the Kings Buildings to dash in and wolf down my dinner before going training. I never had the money but often I recall when I emerged from Graham's door how I regularly looked at a little Reliant Bond Bug parked in Balcarres Street. With my imagination I day dreamed that it was mine. It was basically a two seater but on three wheels. I'd fantasise about buying one of my own. How wonderful it would be at the end of the day to be able to make my own way across town and drive back home in comfort and out of inclement weather all cosy and dry to head back home in relative comfort to Durham Road.

I'll miss travelling out each morning with Grandpa Willie to his wee part-time morning job at Waugh & Son Butchers Morningside Road. And parking the car at Nile Grove whilst I sat and read his Scottish Daily Express before walking along to Graham's to begin work.

We've enjoyed each other's company. Travelling together has eased both our passages.

Turning the negative in to the positive, in combating the ennui at work has allowed me much time to go off on flights of fancy. To think and to dream and to plan how life might be. It's given me the luxury of time to properly reflect on and consider what I really want to do with my life. Having to work all day whilst my peers have been at school and university has made me realise that, yes, I want some of that life too.

Even just simple things. Training with students on Wednesday half days has an enormous appeal to it rather than being hunched over this work-bench so much so it sends an adrenaline shot through my veins making some of the miserable days much more bearable as I lived in an imaginary world of my own making.

The mix of being away from my friends and family at Oxgangs combined with life at Graham's has also made me realise just how important Meadowbank has become in my life; not only for athletics but as the focus of my social life too.

Anyway come August an exciting shiny new world awaits me. I think I can do it. In fact I know I can do it and make it work. Much of that is due to the support to follow my bliss from Mum and Dad as well as the ongoing support from Nana and Gaga.

One other small change is Gaga is going to have to box clever for first read of The Hornet! Up until now he's been mostly in without me about when the paper-boy delivers it on a Monday afternoon. Now he's going to have to fight for first read! The good news on that front is that Wilson is back in the comic from next week in a new adventure. Of course out with Jenkins, Wilson's my real hero!

A lovely dinner whilst reading The Hornet and the added bonus of some lovely Luca's ice cream. A real treat. In the evening I watched the Schools' International. With being booted out of Boroughmuir I was never able to enjoy that great honour. I thought Ann Clarkson was great - a super run and I told her so. She just needs a little more confidence and she could become really very good indeed.

On a less happy note the father-figure of Edinburgh Athletic Club Bert Sinclair died this evening. It came as quite a shock. Even when you're young the death of someone you know halts you in your tracks. Nothing's for ever. And all the more reason to seize the day. And the future too.

Monday 28th October 1974 I posted off a letter to Elaine. My Athletics Weekly still isn't in which was disappointing. Now that I've left work and trying to make something of my life I'm in to a new pattern. With Mum's contribution to help facilitate my studying I bought my monthly bus pass en-route to Telford College. We had our first exam in English. I think I've done okay in it. In the evening we trained indoors at Meadowbank. I was just thinking what a nice girl Alison is. In the evening I watched a good Western, Death of a Gunfighter. It was about the passing of the West. I did some sit-ups and other exercises. Then I went off to bed thinking about Elaine.

Thursday 21st November 1974 Kim Roberts told me 'You fancy Alison!' She's right.

Monday 25th November 1974 I enjoyed a long lie in this morning. It's one of the advantages of giving up work at Graham's and going back to study. My Athletics Weekly was in at Swan's Newsagent's – always a great start to the day. After lunch I went back up to the post office and then out to college to hand in my form before going along to Princes Street to stand in Menzies for a while reading their newspapers, magazines and books. In the evening I trained at Meadowbank. I had an argument with Alison's coach, Stuart Gillies. I really like Alison.

Sunday 4th December 1974 Just before I left for college the phone rang. It was some of Shona's pals having a bit of a laugh. It was a hell of a day outside, absolutely pouring with rain. Come the evening I found my gym session hard going. Later I did a fartlek with Stewart Walters and Alison.

1975

Thursday 2nd January 1975 I rang Paul to go up to Meadowbank to watch day two of the Powderhall New Year Sprint meeting. I bumped into Davie Campbell the physio. I'd taken my tartan rug with me which I shared with Alison. Lovely being snug and close up together. After tea the two of us went along to the physio's: he promised us a bottle of champagne if we're on the telly on Saturday. In the evening I packed my kit for Cosford and had a reasonably early night.

Sunday 19th January 1975 It was very frosty this morning. Heather and Nana are away on a 'stone trip' to the ploughed fields of Fife. After getting in some groceries I phoned Coach Walker and picked him up. I also gave him a lift home. In training I ran a good 300 metres. We were looking at the programme for the Scottish Indoor Championships next Saturday. It should be a cakewalk. Later I gave the lovely Alison a lift home to the Braid Hills.

Toilet

'...I wonder will my mouth open and say
'Are you going all the way
to Newcastle? or 'Can I get you a coffee?
Or will it simply go 'aaaaah'

as if it had a mind of its own?

...A tunnel finds us looking out the window
into one another's eyes. She leaves her seat
but I know that she likes me...'

Hugo Williams

I have a sore throat so I went to bed early.

27th January 1975 The rain was teeming down. Our new kitten Tiki unfortunately looks as if she's heading for the happy hunting ground. Cat heaven. I was given a good headline in the Glasgow Herald for Saturday's double win at the Scottish Championships at Perth. Mid-morning I went along to the physio. Paul arrived halfway through. We went up town together. For 'artistic reasons' we went to see Emmanuele to see what all the fuss was about! Back home I listened to Bryan Ferry's Those Foolish Things album. The title track makes me think of Alison. I lay back idly daydreaming of being her boyfriend. And spending fun outings and lovely days with her.

Those Foolish Things

'...The beauty that is Spring
These foolish things remind me of you
How strange how sweet to find you still
These things are dear me
They seem to bring you near to me...'

Eric Maschwitz

In the evening I trained at Meadowbank. I was high as a kite. Of course I blame the presence of the fabulous Alison. Unfortunately she was there with her boyfriend.

Tuesday 28th January 1975 Travelling home on the bus from college it was still light. It's always such an uplifting moment in the calendar year - if this be winter and all that. I had a really good time at Meadowbank this evening getting on well with everyone. I was running well too. I reckon I could take Alison out. I'm buying her some earrings. I fell asleep listening to Bryan Ferry 'Those stumbling words that told you what my heart meant...'

Friday 31st January 1975 I left home at 8:30 a.m. to head up to Waverley Station to meet Robert Sinclair. Before leaving for Wolverhampton I managed to buy some books, a cassette and a pair of earrings for Alison. The railway journey passed by nicely. It was a smooth trip down through the winter landscape. I ran well in the British Senior Championships. I just missed the final by three-hundredths of a second. I phoned Bill to let him know. Whilst having our meal at the Old Vic Hotel I saw Bob Benn to speak to.

Sunday 2nd February Although I've raced at Cosford the past two days with two quarters on the Friday night and yesterday's 600 metres relay leg (less than a second outside the world best!) and not getting home until the early hours of this morning, I decided to go up to Perth to race a third day. Robert Sinclair drove Stewart Walters, Davie Reid and me up in his mum's large Ford Cortina estate. It doesn't half fly. It was the usual three figures white knuckle ride! It's the Scottish Universities Championships. Roger had a good double in the 300 meters and 600 metres - if we'd raced against each other it would have been interesting over the shorter distance. He ran 35.5 seconds and then 80.9. I ran in two of the invitation races over wildly different distances. I dead-heated with AAA Junior 200 metres champion Drew Harley over 50 metres. We were given the same time but he was given the nod. I was quite happy with the performance as I slipped at the start. Running on what's essentially a concrete gym floor in flats isn't really ideal. But it's good fun. I then ran a big personal best over the half mile. I just sat on Brian Gordon the whole way round. On the tight 150 metres boards and with the short straight I couldn't really move past him but I was quite happy with the run – the quickest by a Junior in the UK. It makes me think what I could run for the distance. I think I could win the AAA Junior Championships 800 metres. But I'm equally confident that I can win the 200 metres and 400 metres so will go for that as a double. I'm actually running so well just now over 60 metres that I feel if I were to just focus on pure speed-work then I could win that too! Gaga picked me up back in Edinburgh. I was thinking of giving Alison a ring but as calibash is rather low I decided not to. Nana Hoffmann sent me a card. I gave my father's wife a ring. I'm to visit her next Sunday.

Monday 3rd February 1975 After a long lie in bed after my exploits over the past three days I picked up the newspapers, went to the physio and then to college. In the evening Gaga gave me a lift up to Meadowbank. I gave Alison a pair of earrings. She gave me a choker in return. I'd have liked to ask her to the dinner-dance but may just have to ask someone else.

Wednesday 5th February 1975 An early lunch before college. After my fantastic running over the weekend I'd been hoping for a letter from the British Amateur Athletics Board perhaps getting my first senior British vest for the match against Belgium. But no joy. College was enjoyable. I was playing table tennis in the common room with several people including the gorgeous looking girl with the long blonde frizzy hair. None of the guys can take their eyes off her. I ran a good session at Meadowbank, had a shower and came home to watch the Scotland v Spain match. It was a 1-1 draw. What a bloody atrocious referee. With Valentine's Day on the horizon I sat down and sketched out a poem for Alison.

Friday 14th February 1975 St Valentine's Day I was up early this morning. I had to take Gaga's car along for its MOT at the Braefoot Garage. I received a large Valentine card this morning. I think it came from Alison although that may be wishful thinking on my part. I had posted off a couple of cards. I met Mum at St James Centre to return the money I'd borrowed from her. I managed to beat the good Swedish table tennis player Anders at college today. I now think I'm better than him. In the evening I took the car out to Oxgangs. I chatted away with Iain and Lucy. We all had some fish 'n chips before settling down to watch Phantom of the Opera, the classic horror story of the mad and disfigured musician who haunts the sewers of Paris and wreaks vengeance on all who thwart his plans.

Saturday 15th February 1975 I received another Valentine card this morning. This one **is** from Alison so yesterday's one was from Shona. The giveaway was the humour, the wit, the intelligence and the charm.

THERE'S JUST ONE THING
A MAN OF YOUR VIRILITY
SHOULD HAVE ON
VALENTINE'S
DAY...

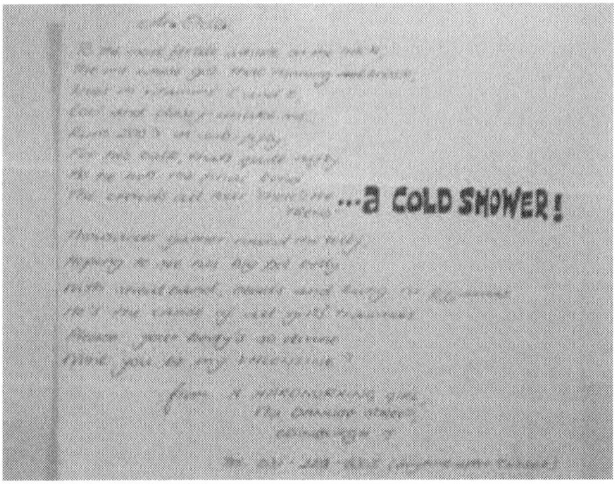
...a COLD SHOWER!

An Ode

To the most fertile athlete on the track
The one who's got the running ~~act~~ knack
Lives on vitamins C and E
Cool and classy-unlike me.
Runs 200's in sub-fifty
For his bulk that's quite nifty.
As he hits the final bend
The crowds all roar 'There's the trend'
Thousands gather round the telly.
Hoping to see his big pot belly.
With sweatband beads and Kung-Fu pyjamas
He's the cause of all girls' traumas.
Please your body's so divine
Won't you be my Valentine?

**From A. HARDWORKING GIRL
17a DANUBE STREET
EDINBURGH 7
Tel. 031-229-6315 (any time after 7 o'clock)**

I felt very sick after this morning's training session. I was chatting with Bob Sinclair, Helen Golden and Ann Clarkson. I collected the fish at Joan Croan Bee on the High Street. I came home to watch the indoor athletics. In the evening Paul phoned but I decided to just stay in. There's a good new series on called The Hanged Man. Nana, Gaga and Heather didn't get in from their event until after midnight – not like them at all. They must have had a lovely time.

Wednesday 5th March 1975 After Geography I headed straight down to Meadowbank in the afternoon. After a little studying Bob and Alison arrived. We had a good laugh. Come the evening I ran a remarkable session.

Wednesday 12th March 1975 My cold is even worse today. I was unable to attend college. I looked into Meadowbank picking Bill up. Paul and I went in to watch the karate international. I enjoyed it despite suffering. Afterwards I gave Paul and Alison lifts to get their busses. I'm feeling so unwell I was unable to sleep.

Sunday 16th March 1975 After my bad cold it was time to check out my fitness after a week off as we begin the countdown to Cosford's British Junior Indoor Championships. I'm still planning to double up. I ended up running a pretty good couple of sessions. It was nice to see Elaine Douglas. She was up from Sanquhar. She wanted my stylish Puma wet-suit top so I gave it to her although it's so different I'd have liked to have kept it for myself. I reckon she wants back off with me. But my heart's set on Alison.

Tuesday 25th March 1975 To the physio first thing and a jog back in the rain. I met Robert at the top of Easter Road before collecting Kim and Dave Hislop and then Alison. We drove through to Glenrothes to the bowling alley. A fantastic evening out including a few drinks not getting back until after eleven o'clock. A fantastic day out with the girls.

Friday 28th March 1975 Robert rang at ten o'clock. Kim then phoned at eleven for twenty minutes. Gaga gave me the loan of his car today so I was able to go out to Oxgangs and then pick up Kim and then Alison from the physio. Later on the car's radiator boiled over but I think Iain's managed to fix it. More taxi-ing dropping Mum and John off at Tollcross before dropping by Bill's for supper.

Monday 31st March 1975 I felt a bit out of sorts this morning but managed the shopping and then breakfast. But after an afternoon session I felt a lot better. Afterwards I took Alison home for tea. A hard session in the evening. After a couple of glasses of milk and a chat with Robert I took the car home.

Wednesday 30th April 1975 No training this evening but I popped into Meadowbank. I was able to give Dave Walker, Dereck Innes and Alison a lift up to the bus station saving them from getting soaked in the pouring rain.

Thursday 8th May 1975 A study day but fine as it poured with rain from morning to evening. After a coffee courtesy of Sandy Sutherland I tried out some new exercises. We also trained indoors. I enjoyed chatting with Alison this evening…sigh!

Monday 2nd June 1975 After the weekend's exploits I've a sore abductor muscle. I visited Davie Campbell the physio at Duddingston Road. Talk about a change in the weather - it was snowing! At Meadowbank I had a slight argument with Coach Walker. But on a happier note after my performance on Saturday I've been selected for the British senior team for the first time for the match in Dresden East Germany. In the evening I went along to Kim's party. It was superb - great fun. I ended up running Jackie; Lynn; Paul; Fiona; Rab and the lovely Alison home.

Saturday 7th June 1975 I wasn't feeling very good this morning but ran an excellent session. Puma sent me some pairs of spikes, trainers and a bag. So along with yesterday's call about Belgrade and my selection for the British senior team in East Germany things are starting to come together.

In the evening Coach Walker; Kay; Robert; Iain; Lucy and Alison and I went through to the bowling alley at Glenrothes. What a fun evening made all the more better for Alison being along.

When You Are Old

'…How many loved your moments of glad grace;
And loved your beauty with love false or true
But one man loved the pilgrim soul in you
And loved the sorrows of your changing face…'

William Butler Yeats

Tuesday 10th June 1975 Well, I wasn't far wrong with yesterday's observation about the laxity of the British Board. I came back from signing on the dole at Portobello to find Nana in a real panic. I was on the phone to their office in London all morning. I was basically just being mucked around. It now turns out I'm not to fly out to Yugoslavia until tomorrow. Every cloud has a silver lining and all that. I went up to Meadowbank. Alison was there but unable to train because of her ankle. Making one of my better moves in life I took her down to Musselburgh instead for a game of pitch 'n putt. It's the first time we've been out alone together since I took her out 15 months ago to the cinema to see It's Only A Paper Moon. We had a lovely evening. We got on pretty well together with lots of fun and laughter. She won by three holes which tells you everything! I'm off to sleep now. To dream about her.

Thursday 12th June 1975 Colin O'Neil very kindly gave me a lift out to Heathrow Airport. He's a lovely guy. Athletics is full of such individuals. Unfortunately I had to wait three hours for a flight home to Edinburgh. I took advantage of the gorgeous weather and lay out sunbathing on the airport rooftop gardens. Nana and Gaga collected me at Turnhouse Airport. They enjoy the wee car run out from Portobello. They had watched last night's race on the telly. It's lovely the way they get some pleasure and return for all they do for me. They're such an integral part of my athletics journey. In many ways it's really a team approach. In the evening I ran a good light session with Graham Malcolm. Alison was down. She too had watched the race. I gave her the Phillips T-shirt which I'd won as a prize. It's analogous to the proud hunter bringing home the spoils!

Monday 16th June 1975 In the evening along with some E.A.C. colleagues I picked up some of the Harvard-Yale guys. We've got a chap called Lance staying over. I haven't taken to him. There's something insincere about the guy. But Grandma Jo is happy so all's good. Alison and I took him and his pal out for a meal. On the way back to Meadowbank we had a great laugh.

Wednesday 18th June 1975 Tomorrow I'm heading off to East Germany with the British senior team for the first time. I met Mum up town and she gave me some money to buy a new shirt for the trip. In the afternoon I did some speed-work with Les Piggott and Scott Brodie. Piggott is an interesting and enigmatic individual. He's quiet but confident and self-assured with definite views on the world. Later on I met Alison at Meadowbank to watch the 3M PRO meeting. It was an interesting experience and the spectacle was presented with flair and razzmatazz compared to the amateur fayre. But many of the great athletes on parade are past their best. Ben Jipcho ran well over two miles. George McNeil was third but not really running at his best. I've been training recently with Jimmy Smith and helping him out but was disappointed with his run in the quarter. Afterwards Alison and I went to Helen Golden's party. Alison went off with DH which pissed me off no end spoiling the evening. C'est la vie.

Age 19

Tuesday 1st July 1975 There were quite a few birthday cards in the post this morning including one from Alison. I was actually supposed to be taking her out but she's got a hospital appointment. As a wee break in training I did a hurdles session. I quite enjoyed it and thought I was reasonable. Elaine Douglas is through for a few days. We're going out tomorrow evening.

Thursday 3rd July 1975 I phoned Elaine this morning to arrange to go out together for the afternoon. We had a lovely time down at Musselburgh and then further down the east coast to Gullane Sands. In the evening I'd arranged to go along to the disco with Alison. She decided that she didn't want to go after all which was a bit disappointing. I instead did some hurdle work in the pouring rain. I was able to see a recording of my Cosford 400 metres race before giving Alison a lift home to Buckstone. After dropping her off I looked into Oxgangs. A nice evening after all including a wee Chinese carry out.

Saturday 5th July 1975 We arrived at Crystal Palace just after mid-day. I made my 400 metre hurdles debut for the club. I ran the second fastest time in Britain for a Junior although I was pretty hopeless in terms of my technique or stride pattern. I also won a fast 200 metres. I couldn't be bothered taking the club bus back to Edinburgh so joined

Bill for the flight back up. It will allow me to perhaps see Alison tomorrow.

Sunday 6th July 1975 An absolute stunner of a Sunday with the sunshine beating down. I ran a good session up at Arthurs Seat. With the weather so fine and hot a large group of us went down to Gullane Sands. The pole vaulter Dick Williamson gave fellow vaulter Dr Mike Bull; Alison; Anne Sowersby and me a lift down the east coast to Yellowcraigs. Bob Sinclair filled a car too, including his sister, Jan, who in the spirit of the afternoon seemed to be enjoying showing off some of her many charms, particularly to the good doctor! Gaga picked me up at Meadowbank. We dropped Iain's girlfriend, Lucy, off.

Wednesday 30th July 1975 I've been taking the kids on the athletics course all week but found it to be a bit boring this afternoon. The build up towards the European Junior Championships continues. I did a very hard session this evening so much so I was away with the fairies afterwards feeling awful. On a happier note I was chatting away with Alison. In the cafe I was talking with Norman Donnachie. He's a good guy - a Borough Road man.

Tuesday 5th August 1975 A pretty easy morning working with the kids at Meadowbank. In the evening I was speaking to Alison. She's really great. Sandy Sutherland gave me a lift home.

Tuesday 12th August 1975 An easy working day at Meadowbank with the kids. Rather than going home at lunchtime I just bought something in the cafeteria. We trained early. I was sick afterwards. The motivation of Athens and the European Junior Championships I guess.

Afterwards Alison and I spent a long time walking around the track together talking. She's absolutely fantastic! Once back home Heather made my dinner.

Thursday 14 August 1975 The hard work leading up to the European Junior Championships continues apace probably witnessed by me not awakening until 10.15 a.m. En-route to my summer job at Meadowbank I bought a birthday card for Alison. Heavy rain all afternoon before running another good session including a superb 350 metres. I'm becoming more and more confident about how I might perform out in Athens. Afterwards Alison and I spent several hours together walking round the track with my arm around her all evening. I gave her a lift home to the Braids. I'm the number one man in her life now. It's only taken about four patient years!

The Passionate Shepherd to His Love

'Come live with me and be my love
And we will all the pleasures prove…'

Christopher Marlowe

Saturday 16th August 1975 From the moment Heather left this morning I spent the next few hours writing non-stop. At Meadowbank I met Alison to give her, her birthday card and present. I enjoyed an easy run in the athletics meeting. Davie Reid came down to stay with me afterwards. We watched the Europa Cup final together. He was actually quite good company.

Sunday 17th August 1975 Less than a week from the start of the European Junior Championships. I'm going well. I put in another good session today. Afterwards I sat around watching a women's athletics match. I spent a lot of the time with Alison. She's absolutely fantastic. The girl for me – marrying material. It looks a good evening for the telly.

Monday 18th August 1975 With Athens in mind I went up to Edinburgh to do a little shopping. A small world. I bumped in to Bob Sinclair and Ann Clarkson. Ann too is on the team for the European Junior Championships. I stopped by at Meadowbank for lunch. I lay out the back sunbathing. I ran my penultimate session before flying out. In my exuberance whilst leaping over a hurdle I banged my knee badly. It's very stiff and sore. It's pissed me off no end given I've been working for this championship for the past year. Alison and I sat and watched the football. We had a good time. I gave her a lift home to the Braids. We stopped off outside the Hermitage of Braid enjoying some kisses 'n cuddles. As we do! Happy days.

Friday 22nd August 1975 Athens I had to get up at 6.00 a.m. which is 4.00 a.m. British time! If you'll forgive the English, the heat starts at 7.00 a.m. British time because of the heat. I was already awake before Malcom Arnold the team coach (t'other team coach is Carl Johnson) came in to Paul and my room. I was hiding behind the door. I leapt out on him giving him an amused shock!

We went down to the refectory. I felt very nervous and found it hard to eat any breakfast at all. We then joined athletes and officials from other countries and took the bus down to the warm-up track which is adjacent to the main stadium itself.

The warm-up track is around 300 metres. It's a brilliant resource in its own right. It has a nice feel to it. I'm quite at home already. Both tracks must have been built for the 1969 European Championships, at least I assume they were.

It was already pretty hot and easy to warm up. For much of the time I remained in the shade. The orange juice sellers were already out. I like the wee bottles of orange squash that they sell.

I was nervous but Malcolm Arnold is a good guy. I found him to be very helpful. I'd drawn the pre-championships favourite Poland's Henryk Galant in my heat so I knew I'd have to run well to qualify. Despite the early hour I felt pretty good. There was a real bonus first thing as my stiff and sore knee had vanished overnight. With Galant outside of me I followed him round the whole way. With four to go through I felt good. We both eased through to the semi-final.

1975 European Junior Championships Morning

(9.10 a.m. - 7.00 a.m. British time!) 400 metres Heat

1. Henryk Galant (Poland)
2. Hoffmann 48.23 seconds

After a warm down and watching some of the athletics I went back on the bus to the university. I had a little to eat and lay on my bed. Of course I couldn't sleep at all. I lay there all afternoon. Paul was in and out as was Brian Jones who'd also qualified this morning. We had a wee game of chess. It's funny although Brian has been my biggest UK rival all year I'm not even contemplating him. I feel there's bigger fish to fry so to speak. It was another of these challenging afternoons. You lie back half thinking about the semi-final and half trying to put it out of your mind. I guess

I'm going to have to get used to this if I want to compete internationally. We kept the windows open. And the curtains half drawn. But it hardly contained the light. There's a dry heat. It's in these moments you find out a lot about yourself.

Late afternoon I got the call to head back down to the track to go through it all once again. Once there I spoke to a friendly young Greek boy who I've been buying the bottles of orange squash from.

The warm-up went fine. I tried to keep to the shade keeping the same routine as this morning including doing my stretching in the shaded foyer area of the small building which has the loos and water fountain. The only small change I made was to dispense with the long white socks. Malcolm was with me again. He's a very re-assuring presence. I'm building a good relationship with him. He likes me. I guess he thinks I've got a little bit character - even if it's just the headband and the early morning fricht! After my strides Malcolm said 'Okay time to go'. He saw me to the tunnel. I walked through to the report area whilst he headed across to the main stadium.

The underground is semi-dark and cooler. We hung about there for 10 minutes before emerging into the bright sunshine and dry heat.

Galant was in the second semi-final which was good news. As we lined up behind our blocks I heard Paul shout out in a long loud drawn-out voice - 'COME-ON BA-BY!'

I couldn't get over how great I felt. I completely cruised around the track. The heat brings out the best in me. Sailing down the home-straight easing off the throttle I just couldn't get over how easy this was feeling so much so that as I glided on to the Finn, Kemola's shoulder I said to him 'Relax...drop your shoulders!' It was a stupid thing to do probably coming across as arrogance but I just couldn't contain my excitement and exuberance. My form is back with a bang!

Paul said there were some great press photos of me. But I wasn't even aware they were available for people to take away. By the time I looked in to the room they were all gone apart from one from this morning's heat which featured Galant and me. He won the other semi-final.

Poor Brian Jones was eliminated. However typical Brian he was very supportive of me. I was so excited about how well I'm running I telephoned Coach Walker. And then Alison. They were both delighted.

1975 European Junior Championships Evening (6.30 p.m. - 4.30 p.m. British time):

400 metres Semi-Final

1. Hoffmann 47.60 seconds
2. Jaakko Kemola (Fin) 47.64
3. Ludger Zander (Ger) 47.88
4. Edmund Antczak (Pol) 47.92

Saturday 23rd August 1975 Athens Food-wise Paul and I have been living mainly off the stuff we bought at the shops. It doesn't seem to matter what meat is served up, it's still swimming in oil. I'm not a fussy eater but again I just couldn't face it. A very easy day trying to stay as relaxed as possible so as not to waste any energy before the final. I played cards in the morning with a few of the guys. I lay on my bed in the afternoon managing to sleep a little. I've just been given a FANTASTIC lift. One of the team officials came to my room with a telegram from Alison sent with love no-less; how my spirits soared!

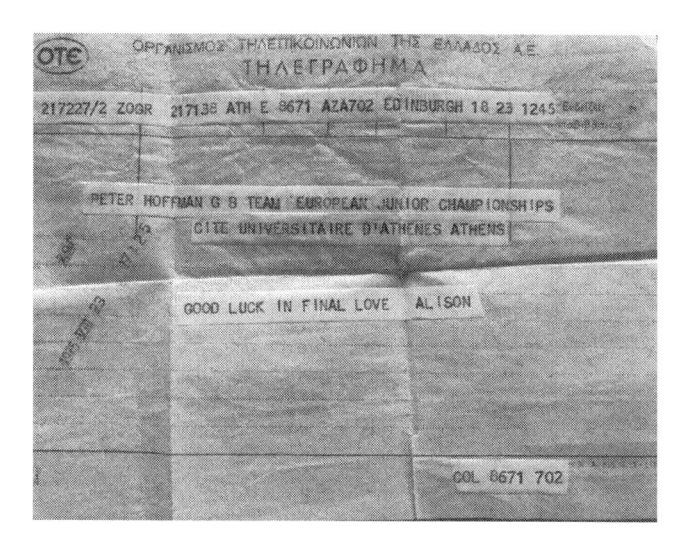

I prepared and re-prepared my bag and kit several times. My G.B. vest is a snug wee fit; the number is 110 and my red Puma Munchen spikes. It was good to get down to the warm-up track to go through the same routine for the third time. I felt okay when I was warming up but not quite as good as last evening before the semi-final when I was flying. However I was very very nervous about the final so I knew that would help me run fast.

Paul said to me that when he was returning on the bus last night to the games village that all the Poles could do was to say Galant and Hoffmann - Hoffmann and Galant. That's given me a lift to know I'm being noticed. It's probably because of the ease of my semi-final run. The great nervousness and worry is a mixture of knowing I'm in with a chance of doing well after last night's performance but the other factor is I don't want to let anyone down including myself.

If

'…If you can fill the unforgiving minute
With sixty seconds' worth of distance run
Yours is the Earth and everything that's in it
And—which is more—you'll be a Man my son!'

Rudyard Kipling

I have to say Malcolm Arnold was brilliant. I said to him that all I wanted to do was to give my absolute best. I didn't want to step off the track feeling I hadn't given it my all. He said he knew I would do that. He was great. He was calm, level-headed, positive and caring - just the right balance.

After warming up it was the same routine. And then once more back into the dark reporting room only to be released like gladiators to perform in front of the waiting crowd. Once again as everyone settled behind their blocks Paul launched in to 'COME ON BA-BY!' At least I was expecting it this time. Galant had drawn lane 1 so I couldn't see him at all but overall lane 4 is a good draw.

The gun fired. I went out reasonably hard but the echelon and stagger remained pretty consistent although I suspect Galant had already moved ahead of everyone. Coming through 300 metres he was ahead. The rest of us were in a line perhaps with Harald Schmidt of Germany slightly up on the rest of us.

Initially I felt disappointed that it was so close particularly as I didn't feel I had much else to give. I tried to stay relaxed. With 50 metres to go Galant was several metres ahead of the field. There was now six of us in a row for the medals. From here I drove on. I just felt I wanted it more than anyone else; that it was more of a fighting spirit than anything physical that saw me through to the silver medal.

If

'...If you can force your heart and nerve and sinew
To serve your turn long after they are gone
And so hold on when there is nothing in you
Except the Will which says to them: "Hold on!'

Rudyard Kipling

I was very very happy especially as I didn't feel anywhere near as good as in last evening's semi-final where I could have registered a faster time. Throughout the race I didn't feel as if I ever quite got going. I seemed to just go through the motions. But when I realised I'd won a European silver medal in a personal best I was absolutely delighted. Indeed the whole team was pleased especially Mike Farrell who had entered Brian Jones and me in the individual event of his own volition so that helped justify his decision. I telephoned home including to the Walker household and spoke to Clint. I phoned Alison's home to pass on the good news to her Mum. If you can't share such moments they're like dust.

The author second right wearing his distinctive headband

1975 European Junior Championships

(6.00 p.m.) 400 metres Final

1. Galant 46.88 secs
2. Hoffmann 47.27 (pb.)
3. Reimann (G.D.R.) 47.41
(9.00 p.m.) 4 x 400 metres relay Heat 2. GBR 3:11.1 (48.1 secs split)

Athletics Weekly Cliff Temple reports from Athens

'...The other British silver went to Peter Hoffmann ranked only eighth before the championships at 400m but coping with three rounds in 36 hours better than most - especially as the first round was held at the equivalent of 7.10 am British time! Hoffmann won his semi in 47.6 and came through strongly for second place in the final in a personal best 47.27 behind Polish winner Henryk Galant (46.88 in lane one). AAA Junior champion Brian Jones never looked happy and went out in the semis...'

Sunday 24th August 1975 Athens The last day of the European Junior Championships.

I spent most of the morning phoning Edinburgh speaking with Alison which was just great. She was delighted to hear about me getting a medal. I also spoke to Coach Walker who kicked off with the immortal line 'What happened!' I also spoke to Nana and Davie Campbell the physio.

Thereafter I relaxed as much as possible.

Come the evening it was back down to the stadium for the fifth and last time. Paul had a disappointing run in the final of the 800 metres but had run well to make the final. Malcolm Edwards was barged off the track in the home-straight. Disappointingly we only finished fifth in the 4 x 400 metres relay running slower than in last night's heat. We were going well half way through lying in second place but Chris Van Rees went a bit mad on the third leg running wide on the first bend and expending so much energy over the first 200 metres that he blew up and struggled to even get the baton to me. If only he'd just sat in all the way and given me the baton on the two leaders' shoulders we would definitely have medalled. Ce la vie. It was surprising given how posh and bright he appears to be. Anyway there was no blame or recriminations amongst us; all I'm doing is recording the facts. I was more disappointed for the rest of the team. It would have been great to see them go home with a medal too. I've already got mine.

However the girls came up trumps. It was lovely to see them get a bronze medal particularly the Scots Ann Clarkson and Karen Williams but the whole team with Ruth Kennedy and Diane Heath are lovely. Ruth did well to just hold off the Belgians on the last leg by one tenth of a second. Later the whole team relaxed.

Early evening the boys had 40 metres races along the university halls of residence corridors. I beat Coe in the final. He's surprisingly quick for a distance runner.

Later on we went to a reception which was just awful. Paul and I were in good form and had everyone in stitches of laughter. Happy days. I'm looking forward to getting home to let everyone see my medal and also to see Alison.

Monday 25th August 1975 Athens Start of College (Telford) In the morning a crowd of us went shopping. I picked up some good T-shirts. The flight to London was fine. Brian Jones and I played chess for much of the journey. I'm very fond of him. He's really looking forward to starting at Cambridge. He has a nice way with him - good humoured, sensitive and bright. I'm sure he'll go far. At London we happened to bump into Frank Dick at the airport for the ongoing flight to Edinburgh. He was returning from the Bank Holiday Monday UK v USSR match. There was a bit of a kerfuffle. He had Ann Clarkson in tears. I jumped to Ann's defence. He told me not to get above myself just because I was a European medallist! For fuck's sake what could you say to that! Bob Sinclair met us at the airport. He gave Paul; Ann and me a lift home. I went out to see Mum. It was FANTASTIC to see Alison again. I ran her home. We stopped off by the Hermitage. As we do!

Tuesday 26th August 1975 The second day of year two of my new routine after 'leaving' work last year. I went into college but found History rather boring. Come the evening I ran a good session with Roger Jenkins and Gus McKenzie. I dominated the eight runs which shows you how much I've come on. For the many unknowing spectators it was three European Junior medallists training together as they'd enjoyed similar success two years previously in Duisburg in 1973. Afterwards Alison and I spent an hour walking around the track having a good chat. Very happy days.

'...Make me immortal with a kiss...'

Christopher Marlowe

Thursday 28th August 1975 I went out to Telford College for the Modern Studies tutorial but discovered I'm unable to take that subject - a bit of a bugger. I felt a bit fed up today - perhaps the aftermath of the highs of Athens? After last evening's good 150s session with Roger and Gus McKenzie I did something lighter. I was running so poorly I've decided not to bother running in tomorrow's Coke Meeting in London. I had a really good chat with Alison. We did our long walk together around the back of Meadowbank because Kim was watching us. I gave her a lift home. As usual we stopped off just past the Hermitage. God she's beautiful.

'...Now a soft kiss-Aye by that kiss I vow an endless bliss...'

John Keats

I was on the end of the most beautiful kiss from Alison. It transformed how I felt earlier in the afternoon. We spent a lovely evening together.

'Close your eyes and I'll kiss you Tomorrow I'll miss you.'

Paul McCartney

Friday 29th August 1975 London Well that will teach me to be spontaneous. After last evening's session I'd decided not to race the Coke Meeting at Crystal Palace but when I awoke this morning in Edinburgh, spur of the moment, I decided to take part. I met the throwers Meg Ritchie and Chris Black at Turnhouse Airport and flew down with them. They're both excellent company. I'd decided not to tell either Coach Walker or Alison to give them the surprise of watching it live on the box and seeing me suddenly appear. I ran surprisingly well running my third best ever time - 47.48. I phoned both of them afterwards. Coach Walker isn't very pleased.

Saturday 30th August 1975 London I was up early this morning to catch a flight from Gatwick Airport to Edinburgh. I felt a bit fed up after the reaction to my spontaneity of racing in London and the adverse reaction to it. I though Alison might have phoned at five o'clock but no luck. I stayed in alone just watching the box. Alison phoned at 10.30 p.m. It was a bit fractious. However Anne Sowersby was very good and phoned up suggesting I come up to the dance and pick them both up. Alison and I stopped off at Arthurs Seat en-route to dropping her home. She's got a sore tooth.

Sunday 31st August 1975 I ran a pretty good session this morning then spent a lovely afternoon sitting out the back of Meadowbank with Alison. Very happy days. Once home to Porty I enjoyed the charming film The Secret of Santa Vittoria. Later Gus McKenzie's dad phoned me with the arrangements for the meeting at Gateshead tomorrow.

Monday 1st September 1975 We (being Mark Wilson; Gus McKenzie and Gus's lovely girlfriend Annette Ramage) left Meadowbank for Gateshead at one o'clock. I didn't run well at all. Perhaps running two hard and fast 300s yesterday probably wasn't a good idea at all as I ran over half a second slower. The minor consolation was I beat Steve Ovett as well as Gus. On the return journey Gus's car broke down at a place called Belford. We had to spend the evening at a bed 'n breakfast. I managed to telephone Alison.

Tuesday 2nd September 1975 Luckily Gus's car was going this morning allowing me to get home by eleven o'clock. Before we left Bedford I phoned Alison at her summer job. I said I would pick her up afterwards. I also phoned my father's wife. She is going to arrange the monthly allowance cheque from Dad to allow me to study for another year to get more Highers to allow me to go to university next year. I picked up the lovely Alison. I gave her a lift home from work and again saw her in the evening down at Meadowbank. I'm drunk on love's summer wine.

Thursday 4th September 1975 I enjoyed Maths today. It's surprising. I'm aware that I need to get an O Level in the subject to be able to apply to universities so it's a necessity. But isn't it strange three years after being turfed out of Boroughmuir School where Maths had been a nightmare.

Now I'm embracing the subject with a passion. Motivation, application and a modicum of ability is a powerful mixture and a potent mix. However, surprisingly given it was my best subject at school (2 O Levels, one in Arithmetic and one in History) I've decided to pack in History. I'm finding the teaching of it so very boring. I informed the college secretary. I have signed up for Biology instead. It's high risk for me as alongside Maths, Science was never my forte. However with my new base knowledge in Anatomy, Physiology & Health and my passion from athletics as to how the body works I've got a good grounding there. There is some overlap with the subjects. It's on the plant side that I'll have to work hard and apply myself. I phoned Mr C. and dashed down for a quick rub. As ever he was interested in how things were going with Alison. He gave me a bottle of wine for the two of us. I've never drunk any wine. I went up to Meadowbank. I picked Alison up. We went off to see a movie. A very lovely evening spent together enjoying each other's company and embraces. Life is so good. I love it. But at other moments worry as to whether our love will last.

Friday 5th September 1975 London I arrived at Waverley Station fairly early this morning to join the E.A.C. team for the Pye Cup Final in Londonshire. I sat next to Alison on the train. The long journey was a joy rather than a bore. From there to Crystal Palace. However a disastrous first day. After my successful debut back in July Coach Walker took the risk of running me in the 400 metres hurdles. I just couldn't get my stride pattern right. I finished last. To round off a terrible evening Roger Jenkins and I mucked up our changeover in the 4 x 100 metres relay. We dropped the baton. We most likely would have won it. That's the first time that's happened to me. It didn't help changing the team's order. Normally I run the first leg. I've always handed over in the lead no matter who I've raced. This time I was on the third leg with Roger on the long second leg.

Alison was furious and in a bad mood on the bus. She said I wasn't to see her this evening. However such is the path of true love - HUH! I wish! We bumped in to each other in the bar. She was in a FANTASTIC MOOD. Being non-drinkers a bottle of wine put us on our backs. We went out for a walk. We spent a lovely evening together.

Saturday 6th September 1975 London It was one of those absolutely lovely soft early autumn days. After breakfast I wandered along to Crystal Palace for day two of the Pye Cup final. The charming Charlie Lipton was along. I spent a little time with him. What a lovely man. John Anderson was there too. We sat and blethered. He was full of praise about me getting the silver medal at the European Junior Championships two weeks ago. 'I told you you would be good'. He's always such a wonderful inspiration. I spent half an hour lying on the pole vault mat with Alison before the 4 x 400 metres relay. She told me if I wanted to spend the evening with her I would have to hand over a 10 yard lead on the first leg. A tall order against the great Wolverhampton & Bilston team full of senior internationalists. Anyway to cut a long story short I ran out of my skin with a 46.8 seconds first leg. Not a bad way to finish off my Junior career. I gave us a 10-15 yards lead. We went on to run a Scottish Club Record of 3:08.9. Pretty good given how young that team is with Paul; Roger; and Norman Gregor. We front ran it all the way. It was a great way to finish off the final. Later John Scott, Lorna Inglis, Alison and I went out for a meal before waiting 90 minutes for the train home to Waverley Station. As ever a turbulent topsy-turvy journey with Alison ranging from hellish to wonderful and all points in between. However it ended all right. We were still pals as we emerged from the train at nine o'clock on Sunday morning. As she said, 'All's well that ends well!'

A Midsummer Night's Dream

'...The course of true love never did run smooth...'

William Shakespeare

Sunday 8th September 1975 Gaga picked me up at the station. I thought he wasn't looking well. It worried me. Despite racing all weekend I was keen to train. I went up to Meadowbank as usual. I rang Alison on a couple of occasions but she was asleep. When I phoned later on she said she was too tired to come out with me. Oh well, if that's how she feels. It's up to her.

Monday 8th September 1975 It was windy, cold and raining all day. Welcome to the festival city. On the way in to college I bumped into Gus's lovely girlfriend Annette Ramage and Norrie Gregor. I continue to enjoy Maths. In the evening I ran an average sort of session. I was delighted to see Alison down at Meadowbank. I spent an hour walking round warming down with her. It's the most fantastic way to warm down after running. We talked and laughed about all sorts of things including her upcoming start as a student at Dunfermline College of P.E. at Cramond. It's all very exciting.

Tuesday 9th September 1975 I was in for Anatomy Physiology & Health and Biology. This DNA business is complex. So much so when I got home I had to have a snooze. In the evening I worked hard in training. Alison and I warmed down together talking about our lives and our hopes with much laughter and kisses and cuddles.

Wednesday 10th September 1975 I was in for just Maths today. After dinner I did a wee session with Alison. It was very cold. So much so I kept my tracksuit on. Ann Clarkson asked me for the £3 I owed her. OUCH! To be honest I'd forgotten all about it. Alison said she'd pay for it which is pretty good of her. I gave her a lift home to the Braids. We stopped off en-route for a baked potato and then outside the Hermitage. A lovely evening together. I feel so happy when we get on as well as we did this evening.

I Love You

'...So kiss me sweet with your warm wet mouth
Still fragrant with ruby wine
And say with a fervor born of the South
That your body and soul are mine.
Clasp me close in your warm young arms
While the pale stars shine above
And we'll live our whole young lives away
In the joys of a living love'

Ella Wheeler Wilcox

Thursday 11th September 1975 The atypical Edinburgh autumn weather continues to disappoint. Horrible wet weather conditions. I ran an average sort of a session. The G.B. girls (up for this weekend's match against Sweden) were out on the track practicing their relay change-overs. Alison and I warmed down together. I gave her a lift home to the Braids via a stopover outside the Hermitage of Braid. I love her. I love these days. I wish they could go on for ever.

Friday 12th September 1975 Although I was in at the main Telford College today I spent a good part of the day thinking about this weekend's G.B. v Sweden international match. However when I drove up to Pollock Halls I discovered that I'm not getting a run. I popped down to Meadowbank to say to Bill I intended running for E.A.C. in the relay instead.

Saturday 13th September 1975 I left Porty quite early to take the roundabout 5 bus up to the Pollock Halls to join the senior Great Britain team meeting for this weekend's match against Sweden. I'm in the relay team but unlikely to run. Last night I told Coach Walker I'd be available to run for the club instead. Afterwards George Sinclair gave me a lift down to Meadowbank. I bumped into Alison. She was smartly dressed in a white jumper and kilt for leading the teams out on the parade. I spent the afternoon with her. She was in a fantastic mood. It was good to see Roger Jenkins win the 400 metres in 46.7 in pretty blustery conditions. Come the evening Alison and I went to the Edinburgh Tattoo. We snuggled up under a tartan blanket before going on to a Chinese restaurant for a bite to eat. Late on I gave her a quick ring to make sure she got home safely. A very happy and lovely day and evening spent together.

Perfect Day

'...Oh it's such a perfect day
I'm glad I spent it with you...'

Lou Reed

Sunday 14th September 1975 I went up to Meadowbank. I was told I'm not to be released to run for the club. Alison arrived just after mid-day. We mucked about all afternoon. Rather wonderfully I got a run after all - my first official British senior vest! When I was warming up with the relay team David Jenkins told me to make sure I was completely warmed up. I don't think he was injured but was just keen to see me get my first British senior cap and to give his brother Roger the glory last leg. I ran well on the first leg handing us over level. The race was incredibly close the whole way round with Roger snatching it on the line by one tenth of a second. Great stuff and wonderful that Alison was there to see it too. At nine o'clock I picked her up at the Morningside clock. We went for a couple of drinks. And then on to the after-match disco. We had a wonderful evening. I'm completely in love and of course very very happy.

Monday 15th September 1975 The day after the dream weekend. It was the Edinburgh Holiday. Three years ago I had been keen to invite Alison out for a mixed game of tennis doubles but of course, being me, had chickened out. It's strange to think that three long years hence we're now girlfriend and boyfriend. After a bath to soak my legs I went out to Oxgangs to visit the family. They'd watched my British debut on the TV. Later I went out to watch Blazing Saddles. What a bloody laugh followed by Enter the Dragon. In the evening I went up to Meadowbank to do a session. Alison pissed me off a little. We walked around the track together after training. She came home with me. I gave her a lift down to Musselburgh.

Tuesday 16th September 1975 I've been given a grant from Lothian Regional Council of £605 to study for further Highers. It's wonderful news. They must have confidence in me. It says much for the city fathers that such a grant scheme is available to people such as me giving me a second chance in life after failing at school. I zipped up to Torphichen Place. I let them know that I've changed some of my courses. After tea I ran a trial with the Edinburgh relay team for this weekend's trip to Munich. I ran a fine last leg storming past Scott Brodie. Afterwards Alison and I spent the evening together most happily! We had a great time and get on so well.

Wednesday 17th September 1975 Only Maths today. Another rainy day. But come the evening a session on my own. Alison came down later and did her session. Afterwards we were chatting away. After training we wandered in to watch a basketball game together. She was in one of her fantastic moods! Which of course made me very happy. But just lovely holding hands together. And then giving her a lift home stopping off down below the Braids lost in each other's arms and embraces and kisses.

Friday 19th September 1975 I couldn't find my passport for Munich. I dashed up to the West End to get a one year version at the Post Office. I rang Bill. Then Nana. And then Alison to update everyone on the situation. When I arrived at Meadowbank it turned out that the manager, Betty Steedman, had my passport after all! What a dolt! We flew directly to Munich arriving there at six o'clock in the evening. Because he was bugging me a bit with all his eggs having double yolks I was taking the piss out of (Drew) McMaster just to take him down a small peg or two.

Sunday 21st September 1975 Munich A touristy day. We watched the Bavarian costume parade before enjoying some lunch at the Olympic Stadium. We then went up the Olympic Tower. I had mixed feelings being there. I'd enjoyed much of the excitement of the 1972 Olympic Games. Whilst up on high I reflected on the tragic massacre only three years ago. Most people went down to the Octoberfest. I didn't really fancy staying so went back to the hostel. I went out instead for an afternoon run with Adrian Weatherhead and Ray Weatherburn through some lovely parts of the city with beautiful houses lining the quiet streets. On such a lovely autumn afternoon it was a joy to be out but I was hanging on for dear life to the boys' coat-tails. I can't imagine any of the other sprinters on the team doing this! Anyway, I knackered myself and ended up with sore hips and legs But I managed to hang in there. I telephoned Alison. It was fantastic to hear her cheery lovely excited voice. I love and adore her. Something beautiful to be flying back to the capital to.

Monday 22nd September 1975 We left the hostel in Munich around 9:30 a.m. to head toward the airport for the flight back to Edinburgh. We had a wee bit of hanging around before it left at mid-day. In the evening I bumped into Alison; a big surprise - she's had her hair cut very short and looks like Mia Farrow. I thought she looked more wide-eyed and beautiful than ever – an image to keep deep in my heart for evermore. We went for a jog come walk around Arthurs Seat, walking hand in hand, chatting six to the dozen sharing the joy of being back together after four days apart. I dropped by Mr C's to make a physio appointment for Thursday.

Tuesday 23rd September 1975 Back to college today followed by an afternoon reading and listening to music. Alison phoned at 4.30 p.m. She was at home at Buckstone. I picked her up and her good friend Wendy from Mary Erskine's who's also starting at Dunf. I drove them out with all their gear to Dunfermline College of PE for the start of their new student life. A new life awaits. I'd like to be as supportive as I can be so was more than happy to be helpful. In fact anything I can do. After leaving them I dropped by Meadowbank. I gave Jackie Groundwater a lift home. It's the least I could do after all the lifts I used to get from her dad, Arthur.

Wednesday 24th September 1975 I was chatting with Laurie Gray at college. Despite it being such a wet wild 'n windy Wednesday evening Alison and I walked around Arthurs Seat before I saw her on to her bus home.

Thursday 25th September 1975 Once again I was just in for Maths today. I wish my grant monies would arrive soon. It was a wild evening. I gave Alison a lift out to Cramond to Dunfermline College of P.E. She took me up to her room. We had a long talk ending up with her telling me she loved me. It was the most fantastic thing I've ever heard in my life. As I drove home I've never felt so happy.

Friday 26th September 1975 When I got home from college it was good to see my grant monies had arrived. Come the evening I dashed out to pick Alison up. With her Mia Farrow haircut she looked absolutely gorgeous - the most fantastic looking girl I ever saw in my life. We went to see The Eiger Sanction. It was okay. We bumped in to another happy couple who are also in love, Helen Golden and Stevie Green. After spending the late Edinburgh hours romantically together we didn't get back out to the college until 1.30 a.m. after a really fantastic evening.

Saturday 27th September 1975 It absolutely poured with rain all day. Early afternoon I met Alison at Binns' Corner. There was a misunderstanding. She'd been standing there for almost an hour. I felt bad about that. We went to see Enter the Dragon. We got in to see it for free. She really enjoyed it. In the evening I met her out at the college. We had an argument. However at the disco we had a really fantastic evening.

Sunday 28th September 1975 the day before Michaelmas I went up to Meadowbank and ran a session on my own. I met Alison at Binns' Corner to do the club sponsored walk together. She wasn't in a good mood, feeling very tired.

Tuesday 30th September 1975 I thought Alison would be down at the track this evening but she wasn't. I was disappointed. I jogged around Arthurs Seat on my own. I felt a bit lonely and sorry for myself. In the autumn you become more reflective.

Wednesday 1st October 1975 On awakening this morning I heard the good news that Ali had beaten Frazier. After a circuit at Meadowbank I came home to watch the big fight. I telephoned Alison at college.

Friday 3rd October 1975 A good day at college. I'm very much enjoying Laurie Gray's company. He's a good lad. In the evening I dropped by Roger Jenkins' for a good blether. I joined him at the Heriot-Watt Student Union at Grindley Street. Despite the charms on display I didn't really wish to be there. I left at ten o'clock to go out to Cramond to see Alison. She had been on my mind throughout the evening; perhaps not my best ever decision.

Saturday 4th October 1975 I went up to Meadowbank for the Saturday morning session. I felt a slight pull in my left hamstring so decided to be sensible for once and didn't train at all. I had a long chat with one of the centre's attendants. I spent the afternoon reading whiling away the hours with the anticipation of meeting Alison later. Come the evening I picked her up to go to see a film. We walked out of it. I was just going to drop her off at the bus stop but thought that would just be daft. Instead we went for a wee drive to Arthurs Seat. She burst into tears. But the evening ended really well with me dropping her off back at her room at college at two o'clock in the morning. Driving home to Portobello I thought how much I adore her.

Sunday 5th October 1975 I picked Alison up at college at eight o'clock. I took her back to our house for a light breakfast. We enjoyed a very lovely day out together at Balloch. Alison ran fantastically well in the cross country at Balloch finishing 6th! I was fair proud of her. Miles and miles better than anything I could do. However she had her purse stolen which was disappointing. Once back in Edinburgh we returned down to the house to borrow Gaga's car. I drove her back out to Dunfermline College of P.E. laden down with pots of Nana's home-made jams, etc. A very lovely day spent together in the autumn sunshine leaving me with a warm glow driving back home to Porty. I went over the day in my mind. All our little interludes, conversations, cuddles and kisses. As you do.

Tuesday 7th October 1975 I was in at Telford College all day made all the better for Laurie Gray's great company. We get on well together and have become very friendly. In the evening Alison phoned me to ask if I'd pick her up. I of course was delighted to oblige dashing off. I happened to pick up Patricia Jones. We didn't have a very enjoyable evening. She was pissing me off somewhat. Blimey, what a rollercoaster. Whilst running Alison back to college I stupidly picked up Pat Jones. I felt obliged to. But not one of my better decisions as it constrained us somewhat with me ending up just dropping them off without even a wee kiss. It left an empty feeling driving home without the security and comfort that comes from ending the day on a happy and fulfilling note. He said with a sigh.

Thursday 9th October 1975 An unusual wee start to the day. I went out for a jog in Portobello Park and Golf Course. I went along to the physio for a rub. Mum had had a bad reaction to some medication so I dropped by to see her before picking Alison up to go to see The Corries. We arrived early. It was great to be able to spend some quality time chatting. The concert was enjoyable. Afterwards I drove her back to college where we sat in the car park at Cramond. We talked for hours not really wanting to say good night to each other. Lovely driving back across a quiet Edinburgh evening on the wings of love.

Sunday 12th October 1975 After just ticking over it was the first day back of track training and the first steps toward trying to make next year's Olympic team. After yesterday's trudge over a terrible but proper cross country course at Galashiels it was good to kick off the day with some group mobility and stretching. In the afternoon Alison and I went up Arthurs Seat together. We had a lovely time just walking hand in hand like many other lovers out on an autumn Sunday afternoon. When we do something simple like this everything in the world feels right and rather wonderful and happy. We enjoyed some of the fantastic views across the city and down the east coast. I dropped her off back out at college. I stopped by Oxgangs for a minute to see the family.

Tuesday 14th October 1975 An enjoyable 'science day' at college. In the early evening I picked Alison up to go training. Afterwards we went up to Arthurs Seat. I could tell she was slightly unhappy. After a while she told me she felt we were becoming too serious. She cried for over an hour. Just to round off a bad day at black rock after I dropped her off at Cramond Gaga's car broke down. Boy oh boy. I managed to get a taxi back home to Portobello. That's what I call a really bad evening.

Wednesday 15th October 1975 A sweet 'n sour day. Well, more sour than sweet. On a beautiful crisp golden autumn morning I ran up to Meadowbank. In the afternoon 'Uncle'

Andy Ross drove us out to Cramond to collect Gaga's car. Andy's a gem - a one in a million bloke who over the years has regularly come to the rescue of Gaga and his temperamental second-hand cars. When we got back home to Portobello, over tea and scones, Grandma Jo tried to give him some monies for his help. Andy said 'Listen if I were to take anything for it, it would take away all the fun I've had; I've had a braw afternoon with Willie and Peter!' I think it's a way for him to do something for Nana and Gaga for the kindnesses which they did for him and Aunt Margaret when they were young and first married. I guess it's an example of Gaga's homespun wisdom - What's round goes around. Whilst I was out Alison had called me twice in the afternoon. I phoned her back at 5:45 pm. Later on, a miserable drunken evening at a 21st birthday party; the ongoing highs and lows of my relationship with the temperamental Alison and my ongoing search for love and belonging. I was pretty upset, but as much for spoiling her evening, which of course she told me. But amongst it all there's training. Always.

Thursday 16th October 1975 Unsurprisingly I felt pissed off this morning. At least when you're in the land of dreams things are fine. Then you wake up to the cold light of day with the early harbinger of a winter without Alison. It may be one long winter going on for years or even decades without her by my side. This is when you need friends. Enhancing my misery, being unused to drinking last evening, I felt God awful physically too. So a double-whammy when combined with my emotional fragility and general dissonance. I struggled up to college. I met Laurie. We went off together to McVitie-Guest at the West End for a glass of orange and a chocolate éclair. He was very supportive – a nice mixture of 'been there – felt pissed off too – played a bad hand – here's what to do'. In the evening I was chatting to Norrie Gregor about my forlorn love-life. He was fantastic. He suggested putting my words into print. With me not being much of a craftsman he volunteered to write it for me. He's had good experience of winning lovers back! Anyway it gave me a great lift. I phoned Alison but she was out at a disco. I instead settled down to watch an excellent new series called Ryan & Macbrayne (Switch).

Friday 17th October 1975 I phoned Alison at half past eight getting her out of bed. Ouch! After a morning at college Laurie ran me out to Dunfermline College. I left the 'masterpiece' letter on her door. I hope she gets it okay. It would be Sod's Law if it ends up going astray. In the afternoon we went off to town to buy some books. Come the early evening I ran a good session with Roger Jenkins before an evening rub at the physio. He's a great guy doubling up as a psychologist. I talked about my miserable love-life. A Friday evening in with Gaga enjoying our fish suppers.

Sunday 19th October 1975 A wasted training day at the Dundee Road Relays. Coming home I dropped by Cramond to see Alison but our relationship is over. KAPUT! I'm pretty pissed off but taking it well.

Monday 20th October 1975 A track session at Meadowbank. I enjoyed a good chat about training and my goals including aiming for the Olympic team. As poor Gaga was off work with pains in his stomach I was able to take the car out to college. I met up with Laurie. He cheered me up no end as we joked about Alison. 'Forget the bitch!' was Laurie's advice. Easier said than done. However despite everything I ran an absolutely brilliant training session. Keep this up and I'll see Montreal.

Tuesday 21st October 1975 In trying to be positive and pointing my life in the right direction I startled even my very slow self by asking out that gorgeous girl who I mentioned several weeks ago playing table tennis. She said yes! She looks like a model. It'll probably only be a one-off date. But still it helps to take my mind off Alison. In the afternoon I trained on my own. I met Alison this evening down at Meadowbank. She's still as gorgeous as ever. Well, how could she ever be anything but in my mind?

Thursday 23rd October 1975 A morning physio appointment. An afternoon of studying. An evening of training. I ran myself into the ground. Perhaps I was masochistically punishing myself for my miserableness at losing Alison. I ended up being absolutely shattered. And sick. I'm unsure what brought it on. Perhaps a hint of Schadenfreude from Alison who annoyed me like never before. What was that all about? What have I ever done to her? However, out of the blue she phoned late in the evening to apologise for her behaviour towards me saying she was sorry. I rang her later. She said she was glad that I did. She'd obviously been upset.

Friday 24th October 1975 I spent the morning at college. In the afternoon I did a session at Meadowbank with Alison who happened to be down. Once again she was up to her nonsense and annoying me. Afterwards I met Roger to run another of our hard hill sessions at Arthurs Seat. We finished just as dusk was falling. I love these Friday afternoon sessions. We work pretty well together. We're pretty much level as we push each other hard on each hill run to exhaustion. Afterwards I enjoy the sense of camaraderie, friendship and shared intimacy as we engage in friendly conversation and laughter and slowly jog-walk back, tired but content, to Meadowbank for a long hot shower.

Happiness

'…They are so happy
they aren't saying anything these boys.
I think if they could they would take
each other's arm.
It's early in the morning
and they are doing this thing together…'

Raymond Carver

Enveloped in the cool air with the temperature dropping like a stone there's the most tremendous blissful feeling of satisfaction. A warm after-glow both physical and mental which emanates from knowing we've hammered ourselves. It's partly the endorphins kicking in. But it's also a joyful serenity that comes from realising and appreciating that our lives have a real purpose. There's something pure about undertaking a shared venture with someone who I like and admire and for which there is no guaranteed outcome.

The rest of the city of Edinburgh carry on with their day-to-day lives oblivious to the extreme and unusual adventure we're on. We're two young men pursuing a dream of Olympia 1976 next summer. A dream across the water. Across the Atlantic Ocean. I feel I'm on an Arthurian quest. Meanwhile at the end of the working week the drivers make their way home snakelike through Arthurs Seat. Their car headlamps light our path back to Meadowbank Stadium.

Somehow being a Friday enhances it all. And the way I feel. As they drive past they are of course oblivious to what we're doing. And of my feelings. And all our fellow athletes throughout the world too, many of whom as **Longfellow** wrote: 'The heights by great men reached and kept were not attained by sudden flight but they while their companions slept were toiling upward in the night.'

Saturday 25th October 1975 I went up to Meadowbank this morning. I ran a pretty good session. Roger Jenkins ran me home. We sat in and watched the Pan-Am Games. Afterwards I lazed back. In the evening I took out the gorgeous looking Miss Angela Watson. Although she doesn't compare whatsoever to Alison we had an enjoyable date. Probably on purpose we just so happened to drop by the party together. Alison was there. She looked good. Very good. I wonder what she thought of me with this drop-dead gorgeous girl on my arm. I hung around just long enough for her to see us before disappearing without speaking to her or introducing Angela keeping this mysterious vision just that – a mystery. I drove her home down the east coast. But I suspect we won't go out with each other again.

Sunday 26th October 1975 The plus or should that be the drawback of us being in the same training squad is that Alison and I continue to see each other. We did a hill session up on Arthurs Seat. Hard work. I noticed that she wasn't feeling too well. She was below par. I went over to chat to her. I couldn't help myself ending up giving her a big kiss. Afterwards I did some weights before joining Paul Forbes; Davie Reid; Mark Wilson and my brother Iain for a meal. We had a great evening with much laughter.

Tuesday 28th October 1975 At lunchtime I went up to the library with Angela no less! She's not only a very pretty girl but very sweet too. I went down to Meadowbank early to get my session out of the way to enable me to avoid seeing Alison. If I wasn't there I thought it might throw her somewhat. Even make her think. At eight o'clock I picked up Paul. We went out to a good sports quiz. I'd said I'd give Bill a lift home. Afterwards I couldn't resist the temptation and zoomed back to Meadowbank to give Alison a lift out to the college. She asked me if I would take her out to see The Way We Were at the Cameo Cinema. We're going tomorrow evening. It's left me feeling much happier returning some hope to my heart.

Wednesday 29th October 1975 We've got a big race coming up on Saturday at Parkhead Glasgow. It's being held at half-time during the Celtic v Rangers match. There will be a capacity crowd to cheer us on.

It's being billed as an attack on the world 500 metres best. But given it's on a cinder surface on the perimeter of the Parkhead football pitch I'll be very surprised. Given the world's number one ranked quarter miler David Jenkins is running I suppose they're at liberty to publicise it that way. It also features Alan Pascoe the European and Commonwealth 400 metres hurdles champion and Bill Hartley the 400 metres hurdler and European Gold Medallist in the 4 x 400 metres.

The distance should suit both of them as they're very strong. Plus there's Roger and Norman so it's a great field. I'm the youngest in the race. Nobody would put their money on me but 500 metres is an interesting distance. I've matched David in training. I'm really looking forward to it. I'm quietly confident of running well. Because the race is at such an unusual time of the year it's meant we've tweaked our training slightly.

As Alison asked me to take her out to see The Way We Were this evening I trained earlier in the afternoon with the university guys. It meant missing college. But it's just a one off. We saw the film at the Cameo Cinema, Tollcross. It was incredibly popular with a long queue trailing all the way around the corner. We just managed to squeeze in getting the very last two remaining seats. Fortunately a very thoughtful person kindly moved their seat to allow us to sit next to each other. The film was quite beautiful. We spent the most wonderful evening together. It made me think. Will we be like Redford and Streisland bumping into each other one day years hence remembering the way we were? I hope not. That would be too heartbreaking.

Sonnet XLIII: 'How Do I Love Thee?'

'How do I love thee? Let me count the ways.
I love thee to the depth and breadth and height
My soul can reach when feeling out of sight….'

Elizabeth Barrett Browning

On such evenings we seem destined to be together. We get on so well. And then for no apparent reason the relationship becomes fragile and teeters on the brink. But tonight was quite unforgettable. I'll remember it always. The way we are, hopefully, rather than the way we were.

Thursday 30th October 1975 Once again I got my session over directly after college. I got away before Alison arrived. However as I got the loan of Gaga's car to collect Nana I picked Alison up and gave her a lift out to college. There was a new series of the excellent series, Switch, on the box this evening.

Friday 31ˢᵗ October 1975 College until mid-morning bumping into John Kerr in town. Later on in the afternoon I was chatting to Dave and Roger Jenkins about Mennea's coach. He's over speaking at the International Coaching Conference. I somehow managed to bump both of the Ford Cortina courtesy cars. I was driving one and Bill was in front in t'other car. I'd only been in it for a second and hadn't had a chance to apply the brakes. As we pulled out of the King James Hotel Bill braked suddenly. I ran into the back of him. Bloody awful! Thereafter I was out with Angela. I'd tried unsuccessfully to get in touch with Alison.

Saturday 1ˢᵗ November 1975 The day of the big race. Because Dave Jenkins is giving a lecture at Frank Dick's annual International Coaching Convention Paul Forbes got a late call up to replace him to make up the field of six internationals. Roger; Norman; Paul and I travelled through to Glasgow together to Parkhead Stadium; Meanwhile Alan Pascoe and Bill Hartley flew into Glasgow from Nice, France.

Because of the religious divide the only instruction we were given by the organisers was to not wear either blue or green in case it antagonised any Celtic or Rangers fans who might throw missiles at us!

We shared the same dressing room as the Celtic players. I was quite bemused at how the 'professionals' prepare for a game. They don't do much of a warm up. And a few of them were enjoying the odd cigarette! We watched a little bit of the game but being 'amateurs' we needed to use the first half to get properly warmed up.

It was quite a challenge as there was only a very limited fenced in area out the back of the stadium. There was only about 80 metres to do some jogging, stretching and strides, rather than the usual large 400 metres arena. It made for an interesting challenge.

It was surprisingly quiet out there. We were shielded from the noise. And then of a sudden a loud roar would arise. Being quite an enclosed area we were all close together. There was some talking. I adopted my usual approach of becoming slightly withdrawn and focusing on what I had to do.

With David Jenkins not running I quite fancied my chances European and Commonwealth gold medallists or not.

Before the race Pascoe gathered us all together. He suggested that because of the tight bends and being a cinders surface that we should forget any world record attempt. Instead we should all run together for the first 300 metres to give the fans value for money. And then it would be everyman for themselves. It didn't affect me one way or t'other. Fast or slow I intended to sit in on the group and kick the last 100 metres turning on the turbo-jets.

Half time arrived.

We emerged through the tunnel in front of 55,000 fans. What an atmosphere. It was an all-ticket sell-out. As the score remained at 0-0 at half-time both sets of fans were in a happy frame of mind. We were introduced to the crowd. A massive cheer went up. I don't think I'd really considered just how close the crowd would be to us - within touching distance.

I was feeling good. I was reasonably well warmed up. The adrenaline was flowing. The gun fired. Pascoe took the race out. Meanwhile I settled in at the back of the group. Although we were running at around 53 seconds pace I was just cruising along concentrating on running the shortest distance. I wore an outfit which I would never normally wear - a t-bar brown vest, white G.B. shorts and my long white socks and headband. Sitting in Wottle-style the biggest challenge was just to be patient.

Half way through Roger Jenkins took the race by the scruff of the neck with a strong burst but eventually faded to fifth. Coming out of the final bend everyone spread out to launch a long drive for home. According to the press I was at least ten metres down on the leader with Paul running well and now holding the front alongside Gregor. Pascoe and Hartley were a stride behind. 80 metres from the tape I put the foot down. I could hardly believe it. Inside 15 metres I easily accelerated past everyone. It was like a knife going through butter. I was still running away from the field at the finish.

Once through the finish line I continued to stride around the bend to acknowledge the crowd. Paul ran well to take second place. Norrie Gregor was third. A victory for Coach Walker's squad and our preparation. Hartley was fourth. Pascoe brought up the rear. Scottish Television (STV) were filming the football match and the race too. Alex Cameron interviewed me track-side. I was still bubbling away with excitement. I said I could easily have kept that pace going for at least another 100 metres. I guess that will be tomorrow's headline. He asked me if I thought I could make next year's Olympic team. With youthful candour and excitement and a lack of circumspection I said 'Yes!' Whilst it puts some pressure on me why not as half the field

- Jenkins, Hartley and Pascoe are all likely to be in the mix for the Great Britain 4 x 400 metres relay team next year.

I'm looking forward to watching a re-run of the race on Scotsport on the television tomorrow afternoon. For winning the race I received an alarm clock and twenty five pounds for travel expenses. Meanwhile Pascoe received five hundred pounds. Ce la vie. One day!

Because we left during the second half we were able to get a very smooth run out of a quiet Glasgow and back down the M8 to the King James Hotel in Edinburgh to catch Jenkins' lecture and interview which I really enjoyed. He's an intelligent reflective individual blessed with enormous talent. He's the greatest natural talent I've come across. And an inspiration to me in many ways. He was genuinely pleased to hear of my win. He said he was unsurprised. Good to have his confidence.

A rather wonderful day was soured slightly later on. In the evening I went out with Alison. She was in a bloody awful mood going off in the huff about her spots. After I'd dropped her later in the evening the Ford Cortina courtesy car which I'd had the loan of as one of the convention's chauffeurs for the international guests ran out of petrol. Given I'd run into the back of Coach Walker's Cortina the night before when he'd braked suddenly it all made for an interesting weekend. I guess you can't have everything in life. A full on day.

Monday 3rd November 1975 College was a bore today. I did an easy sort of a session. Surprisingly Alison was down at Meadowbank this evening. She said how glad she was to see me. I gave her a lift out to college where we spent some lovely hours together. I love you. I love you. I do.

Wednesday 5th November 1975 I joined Laurie for a highly enjoyable game of squash at the Edinburgh Club in the Dean Village. Come the afternoon I picked up some new cassettes and helped Gaga out taking him up to Edinburgh. In the evening I picked up Alison. We went to see Love Story. We had a lovely time. Back out at the college we fell out. And then we fell back in ending the evening on a high. Despite the ups and downs I drove home feeling happy.

Thursday 6th November 1975 Whilst in at college this afternoon I tried to phone Alison. But no luck. An evening training session. As I didn't have the car Alison and I hung around together squeezing each minute from the hour or so before we had to go our separate ways. Whilst at the bus stop I was chatting with Lorraine Morris.

Friday 7th November 1975 A fine college day followed by a good afternoon training session at Meadowbank. Alison was there. I gave her a lift home before dropping by Oxgangs. I dropped Mum and John off at the Firemen's Club before a quiet evening in by the fire watching the box.

Sunday 9th November 1975 A lovely frosty morning out. Before and after breakfast I studied until the church bells rang out. Grandpa Willie gave me a loan of his little white Ford Escort with the go faster Mexico thin red stripes. I was able to take some of Coach Walker's squad down the East Lothian coast to Gullane to train on the sands.

Big Norrie sat in the front. We were able to enjoy some good craic. Anne Sowersby, Linda Waite and Alison were able to blether away in the back.

The weather was glorious. It was crisp and cool. The sun shone all day. As ever it was great fun. We had a fantastic workout.

Coach Walker led us on the usual fast jog warm-up run before we did a variety of stretching; sprints; bounding and then an Indian relay along the shore to finish the session as usual with an intensive and competitive relay race on the Big Dipper dune. For most of us we reach that point where your legs just give way. You just collapse on to the sand.

The terrain is a great leveller. Athletes who I might normally out-run quite easily on the track can be surprisingly close to you on the beach sands. That natural spring which gives you an advantage is taken away. Instead it becomes solely a matter of raw strength. A few of the athletes were sick. I tend to feel sick and dizzy with the usual feeling of a burning lactic sensation. However I don't feel the same intensity and nauseousness which you get from a longer flat out effort on the athletics track.

Coach Walker is smart getting everyone working hard through a subtle peer pressure by organising us into team relays. The athletes end up going the extra mile and pushing themselves harder than they might otherwise do so. And it's all within a fun environment with your team-mates cheering you on. And of course it's all taking place within the glorious setting of golden sands, a clear blue sky and sea.

At the end of the two hour session I ran into the cold winter sea for a quick splash and cold dip. I was just showing off. As usual. Thereafter we trudged back up to the car park. We headed back home to the capital via Musselburgh and

Luca's ice cream shop, the finest in Scotland. We all stopped off for a slider or a tub of Italy's finest export.

After dropping off the others I gave Alison a lift home. On this Sunday afternoon we're still in love. We sat in the car for a couple of hours enjoying magical moments together. A lovely and memorable day. One not to be forgotten. Later in the evening I joined Davie Reid and Mark Wilson for a meal out.

Tuesday 11th November 1975 A difficult day. After college Gaga gave me the loan of his car. I went up to Meadowbank to train. I wasn't running well. Coach Walker and I had a major fall-out. As you might expect I was told in no uncertain terms that I needed to pull the finger out. And if not perhaps I should consider looking for another coach. So I'm feeling pretty fragile at the moment on that front not to mention the roller-coaster ride with Alison. There's a basic fragility and insecurity at the heart of me. Whilst I may come across as someone who is confident and out-going with a lot going for me, perhaps even a little bit cocky I don't think I'm brash in say the Drew McMaster class as I'm sensitive to others' moods and needs. And whilst I've been described as cocky in newspaper articles it's really just a joie de vivre at winning races. After giving Anne Sowersby a lift home en-route I drove out to Cramond and Dunfermline College of P.E. Alison and I sat for several hours having a lovely conversation. God she's so beautiful. I love her so much.

Sonnet 18: Shall I compare thee to a summer's day?

'Shall I compare thee to a summer's day?
Thou art more lovely and more temperate:
Rough winds do shake the darling buds of May
And summer's lease hath all too short a date;
Sometime too hot the eye of heavan shines
And often is his gold complexion dimm'd;
And every fair from fair sometime declines
By chance or nature's changing course untrimm'd;
But thy eternal summer shall not fade
Nor lose possession of that fair thou ow'st;
Nor shall death brag thou wander'st in his shade
When in eternal lines to time thou grow'st;
So long as men can breathe or eyes can see
So long lives this and this gives life to thee.'

William Shakespeare

Wednesday 12th November 1975 An early morning game of squash with Laurie. A very good competitive match with him just emerging as the winner after a titanic struggle. For a newcomer to the game I've come on rapidly. For the rest of the day I studied and listened to some music including a beautiful cassette by Michael Jackson. At twenty to eleven in the evening I phoned Alison. We had a really good long chat.

Thursday 13th November 1975 Mr C's for a rub. The bank. The record shop. And then Maths at college. I trained on my own. With no coach it's going to take a lot of self-discipline if I want to fulfil my dream of making the Olympic team. Once home I tried to phone Alison from around twenty past eight onwards. It's pretty challenging trying to get through on a public phone that serves all the students. A disappointing conclusion to the day with not being able to speak to Alison.

How my true love and I lay without touching

'How my true love and I lay without touching
How my hand journeyed to the drumlin of his hip
My pelvis aching...

...and I aching
in our cold single beds with many seas dividing
as we think of the years that we spent without touching.'

Leland Bardwell

Friday 14th November 1975 College all day. Followed by dinner. But no training. I'm down with a cold. At five o'clock I picked up Alison. We went round to Mum's for tea. Afterwards the two of us went in to see Lynn Kerr. She's been in the Edinburgh Hospital at Morningside suffering from anxiety. Thereafter we spent a wonderful evening out at Cramond listening to records and loving each other. Alison ended up with no clothes on, naked as the day she was born. She was slightly embarrassed about her body. I thought she was wonderful. And quite beautiful. I drove home on the wings of love. What an up and down period this has been. But I'm feeling much happier and positive about our future together. I'm head over heels in love with her. As the cliché goes.

Sunday 16th November 1975 Alison and I travelled down to Hawick for the cross country. We didn't get on too well. Something is spoiling things and our relationship. And it's definitely emanating from her. I'd love things to work out between us. It's such a contrast to the love we showered upon each other just the other evening. It leaves me at a loss. I'm not the most secure person. I find everything so stressful and worrying. I long for a stable loving relationship with her. Is that so hard and beyond us. I just wish to spend endless happy hours with her. It's what we should be able to do at this lovely stage in our lives. Outside it's damp and cold. I long to be in bed beside her. Cuddling and kissing.

Monday 17th November 1975 I spent a good part of the day reading David Niven's highly entertaining The Moon's A Balloon. Quite late on I looked in to Paul's party. Alison was in a foul mood but snapped out of it slightly later on. I was able to give Fiona Hunter a lift home.

Tuesday 18th November 1975 I had some exams today. I've probably passed APH (Anatomy, Physiology & Health) but failed miserably in Biology. I went up to Meadowbank. I had a couple of hours chat with estranged running coach Bill Walker. Afterwards I went up to Meadowbank. I picked up Alison. She was in a terrible mood. We ended up having a bit of an argument. Well, at least a one-sided one. She gave me a telling off. I've decided that for the next few weeks we should have a break from each other. But, I can see it being much much longer. It makes me sad.

Thursday 20th November 1975 Maths was most enjoyable today. In the evening at Meadowbank Bill Walker more or less ignored me. Still, I ended up working hard in training giving the Pros a good start and chasing them down. Alison and I had a small civilized chat. Taking my mind off the fact that two of the three main strands in my life's existence are crumbling away I began reading a new book late on in the evening.

Friday 21st November 1975 I had another Biology exam which I failed miserably. I also failed AP&H. I ended up going for a drink with Laurie Gray. I'm failing now on all three fronts – love, athletics and my academic quest too. I bumped into Anne Sowersby and former primary school 'girlfriend' Audrey Smith. I ended up phoning Alison to see if she might want to go out on Sunday evening. She's agreed. But I had to persuade her which isn't a good situation. It signifies the writing is on the wall. It's best to forget her. I've done it once before. I can do it again. I've bought three new books to while away the lonely winter evenings. On the way home I stopped off at the Edinburgh Club. I've decided to do some karate. I had a pint of beer. I stayed in to watch the TV. Friday's viewing is usually pretty solid.

Saturday 22nd November 1975 Despite a general dissonance and completely blowing up on the last run I ran an excellent training session this morning. I'm taking it as a positive. I've pushed myself pretty hard. I felt particularly good early on floating through the first half of the session. In the afternoon I warmed down with a saunter up to the Scottish Cross Country Relays to watch the iron hard men of the iron hard ground. I spent the evening reading. I resisted the temptation to phone Alison - 'manfully' succeeded. Just!

Sunday 23rd November 1975 Coach Walker and I haven't patched things up since we fell out. I'm mostly training on my own. It's not ideal particularly if I'm aiming for Montreal. It's certainly a wakeup call and causing me to reflect on things. First thing I wandered up to the karate session at George Kerr's Edinburgh Club at Hillside Crescent. Well that was an interesting session. Immediately afterwards I went straight down to Meadowbank. I ran a solitary session. It wasn't much to write home about. However on a very lovely late autumn day an upbeat afternoon. Alison and I walked the dog for a few hours up on Arthurs Seat. After collecting Nana and Aunt Heather from Waverley Station I enjoyed watching A Streetcar Named Desire. My cultural education continues apace.

Tuesday 25th November 1975 Spur of the moment. On passing Interflora I decided to send Alison some flowers. Outwith thinking of her, an ordinary day, if there's such a thing these days. I feel all at sea. I went to college. I saw my brother Iain for a second. I did a reasonably hard training session on my own. I sat in front of the telly all evening thinking about Alison. At times I wondered if she'd received the flowers okay.

Wednesday 26th November 1975 Maths was enjoyable today. My new found enthusiasm for the subject continues. Come the evening I went along to karate training. I enjoyed it. The instructor is very good and a nice guy with it. Before bed I enjoyed some fish 'n chips. I thought that Alison would have phoned me after sending her flowers but I sat forlornly by the phone – she didnae phone!

Friday 28th November 1975 I took a tracksuit in to college to give to Laurie. In exchange he's given me a rather attractive harlequin Gordonstoun School hockey shirt. I got my Biology results back – 16%. I'll have to get working. There was a phone call from Alison this evening. A big 2p's worth. I hope she could afford it. An evening karate session before taking Iain's birthday cake out to Oxgangs for tomorrow.

Sunday 30th November 1975 An early session of karate at the Edinburgh Club before an average track session alone. But by no means poor. A few of us watched a karate demonstration at Meadowbank in the afternoon. For around three-quarters of an hour I felt slightly depressed with the thought of the ethereal Alison slipping out of my life. A friend happened to call in the evening. It cheered me up. I watched the Sunday film and read till late on helping to keep thoughts of Alison at bay.

Monday 1st December 1975 College. The rain poured down incessantly all day adding to the general miserableness. It was very cold. And dull. And overcast. Gloom. And further gloom. After a reasonable solitary session my resistance collapsed. I dropped by to see Alison. It of course wasn't a good idea. Still.

Thursday 4th December 1975 Maths was good. I was running well. Two positives in my life. However Anne Sowersby says that I've to finish with Alison on Saturday. She says I'm too much for her. I just don't know what to do. I was just settling back with a book to read when Alison phoned me out of the blue.

Friday 5th December 1975 The ever supportive Laurie Gray advised me to 'Say nothing to Alison; if she wants to end it all then it's up to her'. I agree. Why should I end it when she means the world to me? Late afternoon just as dusk was falling Roger Jenkins and I ran a hill session up on Arthurs Seat at the 'Holyrood Bowl'. We were both pathetic. We're both feeling buggered just now as we continue our training towards the dream of Montreal and the Olympics. Davie Reid phoned me. I picked him up to go to the E.A.C. dance. Oh, one piece of good news – two pairs of spikes arrived in the post today from Puma – a pair of Jumbo and a pair of Munchen '72.

Saturday 6th December 1975 I was up relatively early today because we needed to start the session at Meadowbank at 9.45 a.m. On arrival both Coach Walker and Roger Jenkins immediately put my back up annoying me. At lunchtime I met Alison. We went to Murrayfield to watch Scotland beat Australia 10-3. Taking Laurie's advice I decided not to say anything. She brought the subject up briefly. In the evening Davie Reid came down for a game of chess, a bite to eat and a blether before we went up to Meg Ritchie's party. Not being interested in any other girls I didn't feel like staying long. I came back home early. I went to bed with Agatha Christie's 'Dead Man's Folly'.

Monday 8th December 1975 I stocked up on my sleep lying in bed until ten o'clock. I gave Maths a miss today. I phoned Mum to say I had a Puma shoulder bag for her. I bought Portrait in Motion by Arthur Ashe as Alison's Christmas present. I ended up reading it myself. Roger Jenkins was down. We ended up doing a hill session together. Come seven o'clock I returned The Way We Were album to Alison. She wasn't in at first. I looked by the Cramond Inn for a half pint of beer. I sat reading Agatha Christie's Elephants Can Remember. She was there at nine o'clock. It now seems that I'm only to take her out occasionally. Back home I enjoyed Ned Kelly particularly the songs and the lyrics.

Tuesday 9th December 1975 Ouch! An early 7.15 a.m. rise on a December morning. Another wee surprise with the post this morning. Another parcel from Puma. I'm being bombarded. It included an interesting variation of previous pairs of spikes sent to me. This time Puma Munchen top but Puma Jumbo sole. Interesting. Different. There was also another small Puma top which I'll give to Alison for her

Christmas. In 1973 I wrote in my diary I wonder if Alison fancies me at all. I spoke briefly with Iain this morning. I spent much of the day reading Arthur Ashe's Portrait in Motion. I also managed to read a chapter of Biology. I've set myself a couple of goals over the festive season: (i) get lots of studying done to kick start the process of getting some good Highers next May; and (ii) reduce my weight – crikey, I'm 10 stone 10 lbs!

Wednesday 10th December 1975 I was up to Benson's early this morning. I got in Nana's messages before helping 'The Bookie' to start his car. I ended up pushing it by myself all the way down Durham Road. I was absolutely shattered. In future I'll be careful about doing something similar. It could be quite dangerous. I was beaten again by Laurie at squash. But with my fitness I won the last few games. If I were to play regularly I think I could be very good indeed. In the evening I did a tough circuit. I ended up coaching eight young Edinburgh Southern Harriers who had turned up to train but there was no coach there. I didn't want to see them disappointed. I enjoyed myself finding it very satisfying to make a small contribution. But it's not something I would wish to do. At least not just yet. I completed the Arthur Ashe book. I found the diaries the best part. I saw my first lit Christmas tree in a window on the way home. It's always a lovely moment taking me back to being young counting Christmas trees with Anne and Iain from Gaga's car. Steele won the BBC Sports Personality of the Year. Disgusting. It should have been Edinburgh's David Wilkie.

Thursday 11th December 1975 I visited Mr C. for a rub this morning. It was good to see him. He recommends seeking out Alison to arrange something over the holidays. But I just don't know. I've no enthusiasm for chasing up girls. It's just not worth it. Is it? All that pain and angst and uncertainty. In the evening I was able to join Bill Walker's squad for the first since we fell out. I was running well giving them something to think about. I sat chatting with Bill in the café until 10:30 p.m. I suddenly remembered I was supposed to have phoned Shona earlier this evening. After a quick shower I grabbed some pie and chips.

Saturday 13th December 1975 I was out to see a couple of good Clint Eastwood films last evening with Shona. But I won't take her out again. It was cold this morning. But at least it was dry. At Meadowbank I bumped into three of my former Oxgangs pals. I ran a very good session but felt bloody awful afterwards. Even now at half past midnight I've still not fully recovered from pushing myself so hard. After yesterday's titanic and tense victory against Laurie I spent the rest of the day working on a chess problem. I had a bad lapse around five o'clock. I rang Alison at her home. But fortunately she was out. On reflection I was probably fortunate. A lucky escape from further disappointment. Bill Walker returned the film tapes. Tomorrow I'll give Gaga's car a wash and a clean.

Sunday 14th December 1975 I washed Gaga's car first thing. Despite not feeling well I ran a remarkably good session. In the afternoon Paul Forbes and Mark Wilson came down to the house to watch a film. But the video wasn't working properly. I was thinking about the upcoming 600 metres race at Cosford in January. The session wasn't one that I enjoy. It was too open-ended for my liking. I much prefer a set distance where I can more accurately distribute my effort. In each of the runs I felt I could still have kept running on at a similar pace which was indicative of me not running quite flat out. Also I had to run the whole session from the front too which again is not my forte either. The weather was cold, wet and windy which makes it look even better. The session comprised of: 90 seconds run (I covered 670 metres); 50 seconds (413 metres); 40 seconds (325 metres); and 24 seconds (215 metres) all with a 12 minutes recovery. In the evening Davie Reid came down to visit me. We watched an athletics programme about the Kenyans. I was quite surprised to see myself appear within the programme. They showed a race clip of the 400 metres at the Invitation AAA v Borough Road College meeting at Crystal Palace back in June where I finished second to Kenya's Stephen Chepkwony. It was after that race I knew I could run well at the European Junior Championships in August.

Remember

'…Remember me when no more day by day
You tell me of our future that you planned:
Only remember me; you understand
It will be late to counsel then or pray.
Yet if you should forget me for a while
And afterwards remember do not grieve:
For if the darkness and corruption leave
A vestige of the thoughts that once I had
Better by far you should forget and smile
Than you should remember and be sad.'

Christina Rossetti

Monday 15th December 1975 Overnight I took a really severe cramp in my right calf. It was bloody agony. I ended up going along to see Mr C. the physio. He offered me some fatherly advice not to phone Alison, but just to just forget her and see if she contacts me. Huh! Some hope of that. In the evening whilst resisting the temptation to phone her I watched a Dustin Hoffman/Mia Farrow film called John and Mary. God she's like Alison with the added irony of a mix of our heroes' names - Farrow and Hoffman. Oh no, an early rise tomorrow.

Tell me not here it needs not saying

'…Or marshalled under moons of harvest
Stand still all night the sheaves;
Possess as I possessed a season
The countries I resign
Where over elmy plains the highway
Would mount the hills and shine
And full of shade the pillared forest
Would murmur and be mine….'

A. E. Houseman

Tuesday 16th December 1975 I went out to college and spent the morning there. Once back home I decided to go and see Alison. I phoned her. I arranged to pick her up at five o'clock. I did. She says she can't go out on Saturday. Or next Wednesday. So I guess I've finally got the message. We were out together on Tuesday past. When I suggested we might meet up come the weekend or this Wednesday she said she was too busy. I guess I've got the message.

As she stepped out of the car I asked 'Where did I go wrong?' She said 'Peter...nothing...you did everything right.'

God, I was pretty upset crying in the car as I drove back.

But I was pleased with myself because I managed to pull myself together and somehow managed to run a half-decent session at Meadowbank.

Lorna Inglis put it in a nutshell.

She said 'Peter, you were lovely to her and she really likes you – but she doesn't love you'.

So, it's over.

It's been a roller coaster ride over the past couple of years with the most delicious and delightful highs as well as some lows thrown in there too. She's not someone I'll ever forget - from our first kiss at the Carnethy Hill Race disco almost two years ago whilst dancing to The Hollies The Air That I Breath. My first, my true love.

On a happier note to finish the most awful day, a small ray of hope – Bill's got me an invitation to the big 600 metres race at Cosford. I'm not only intending to win it, but I want to break the world's best time for the distance.

Twelve Songs

'…The stars are not wanted now: put out every one;
Pack up the moon and dismantle the sun:
Pour away the ocean and sweep up the wood.
For nothing now can ever come to any good.'

W.H. Auden

Postscript

Wednesday 17th December 1975 The morning after the evening before. I sat about all morning mulling over things. It occurred to me that Nana's attic could be converted into a bedroom which would be quite exciting. Maths for an hour. Then I went to see Black Christmas with Davie Reid. He conned me with regard to the cashews. It annoyed me. I don't like seeing meanness in people. Later I watched Isaksson run away with The Superstars title. I read Everest the Hard Way late into the night. It's damn good. (Dougal) Haston's pretty fantastic. I've just noticed that my Higher exams in May clash with the two away British internationals in Kiev and Split. Damn annoying.

Sunday 21st December 1975 I looked into Meadowbank. Alison was there. She gave me a Christmas card and a present of a medallion. Afterwards Norman ran me home. I watched John Wayne in The Alamo before going out to Oxgangs to collect my bus pass money. I stayed until seven before an evening watching the excellent Captain Poldark and Anne of the Thousand Days with thoughts and images of Alison occasionally dancing across the screen.

1976

10th January 1976 Athletics Weekly Report Phillips Cosford Games:

'The men's 600 proved to be a slowish race although rather more competitive than anticipated. David Jenkins had hoped to run the first 200 in about 24.5 the second in 25.5 (50 at 400) and the last in 27-odd. The final lap was covered in 27.2 as it turned out but the initial pace was far off what was required. Jenkins and Ainsley Bennett were abreast at

200 in 25.6 ('that shows a diabolical lack of speed' muttered Jenkins) while at 400 reached in 52.5 Jenkins was a stride ahead of Bennett with Peter Hoffmann a similar margin behind Bennett. The young Scot overtook Bennett halfway round the last lap and started closing on Jenkins but the final result was never in doubt. Hoffmann the European Junior silver medallist ran splendidly even if he was disappointed with his time. Having run the distance outdoors at Meadowbank in very cold weather recently in 78sec he had hoped to duplicate that time in the warmth of Cosford. His target for 1976 is to lower his best 400 mark (47.27) to around 46.5 as well as running a few more 800's.'

Saturday 14th February 1976 St Valentine's Day Alison should have received the flowers I sent.

Tuesday 17th February 1976 With Alison breaking my heart back in December I thought I should take some positive steps forward rather than pining away. I was chatting with Fiona Macaulay this evening. I gave her a lift home after training.

Wednesday 18th February 1976: There was a letter in the post:

Dear Peter

I had to write you a note to thank you for the flowers - they were absolutely super. I wasn't at home when they arrived but my Mum phoned me and I went up on Sunday night to collect them. Not only did the flowers make my day but they made my Mum's as well - she was over the moon!

I must apologise for not sending you a card at least but I have no excuse really except that due to my financial situation I decided not to bother sending any at all. I hope you don't think it's because I've forgotten you because I haven't.

I hope you are still training well and I am keeping my fingers crossed that I will see you at Montreal. I watched your run at Cosford and although you're no doubt disappointed I hope you're not unduly so as perhaps it's best to have your <u>only</u> defeat now and use it to push you harder. For God sake don't allow it to upset your training etc. although I'm sure you wouldn't with a split time of 22.3 seconds and despite this not feeling tired at the end - it cannot have been a bad defeat.

I hope your family - including the cat and dog - are all well and I'll perhaps see you if you go to the E.A.C. disco.

However until then,

Yours faithfully

Alison x

p.s. I'll give Lorna The Moon's a Balloon for you. Sorry it's been so long.

During the session I felt shattered but it's a good start to me working very hard in every session. My new philosophy is to attack every session right from the gun. I'm feeling a bit low this evening. There was another letter and card in the post from Oslo from Bjorg Larsen. She included a nice photograph.

Wednesday 3rd March 1976 A bad day at black rock. I had to drop out of this evening's session halfway through with a bad right Achilles tendon. Later I went along to the

Edinburgh Athletic Club St Valentine's Dance. Alison was there. It's the first time I've seen her since last year. Whilst the dance was fine I went home on a bit of a low feeling a bit depressed that the world's moved on leaving behind poignant memories of the way we were.

Let me not to the marriage of true minds

Let me not to the marriage of true minds
Admit impediments: Love is not love
Which alters when it alteration finds;
Or bends with the remover to remove.
O no! it is an ever-fixed mark
That looks on tempest and is never shaken;
It is the star to every wand'ring bark
Whose worth's unknown although his weight be taken
Love's not Time's fool though rosy lips and cheeks
Within his bending sickle's compass come;
Love alters not with his brief hours and weeks
But bears it out even to the edge of doom.
If this be error and upon me prov'd.
I never writ nor no man ever lov'd.

William Shakespeare

Thursday 4th March 1976 With both Achilles tendons giving me gyp I still couldn't train. However after feeling so depressed at seeing Alison for the first time in three months I felt I needed to do something positive. As an antidote to moving on I went up to Meadowbank specifically to ask Fiona Macaulay out. She said yes. I've arranged to meet her on Saturday. I gave her a lift home.

Friday 5th March 1976 After college and cleaning Gaga's car I went to the physio. He suggest I play things cool with Fiona.

Thursday 22nd April 1976 After being at the physio Roger phoned. We ran a light session. Alison was at Meadowbank this evening. She looked beautiful.

The Avenue

Who has not seen their lover
Walking at ease,
Walking like any other
A pavement under trees,
Not singular, apart,
But footed, featured, dressed,
Approaching like the rest
In the same dapple of the summer caught;
Who has not suddenly thought
With swift surprise:
There walks in cool disguise,
There comes, my heart.

Frances Cornford

I got to bed at 10.00 p.m. tonight. Good boy.

She Walks In Beauty

'She walks in beauty like the night
Of cloudless climes and starry skies
And all that's best of dark and bright
Meets in her aspect and her eyes…'

Lord Byron

Sunday 23rd May 1976 I ran a solid session before settling back to watch the women's East v West match. I had lunch with Alison. I've hardly seen her this year. She's more beautiful than ever. She was encouraging me to make the Olympic team. I said it wasn't looking promising. In the evening Fiona and I went to Inverleith Park. And then back to her home to watch an enjoyable Tom Courtenay film 'Otley' followed by England v Brazil. The Canarinhos scoring in the last minute.

Wednesday 16th June 1976 There was a fabulous congratulations card with love from Alison in this morning's post. I too didn't need the trampette! On the back of the card there was a wee note from her too.

Congratulations!
love
Alison x

Dear Peter

I was on the point of jumping on the trampette when Elaine Davidson told me you'd made the team and after that I didn't need anything to give me elevation because I was so happy for you. I phoned but you weren't in so I thought I'd send the card.

I am really really pleased and as you have worked hard despite setbacks (cough) and I hope that you take Montreal by storm.

Yours Alison x

Alison, centre

Age 20

Saturday 31ˢᵗ July 1976 Montreal A lovely start to the day. There was a telegram from Alison wishing me good luck. But unlike last year's telegram in Athens before the final of the European Junior 400 metres with the relay team having been knocked out yesterday it tasted dry as dust. Even more so after watching today's final with a medal going a-begging in 3:02:0. A bit of a sickener. I swapped vests with Benny Brown one of the American runners who I've become friendly with. Like me he qualified fourth in the US Olympic Trials. But of course unlike me he ran today. Their system is much more straightforward. They just run the first four from the trials. Today I wished I'd been an American. But I was pleased to see him so happy. I admired Walker's win in the 1500 metres. Frank (Clement) was frustratingly close to a medal.

The sunlight on the garden

'The sunlight on the garden
Hardens and grows cold
We cannot cage the minute
Within its nets of gold…

…And not expecting pardon
Hardened in heart anew
But glad to have sat under
Thunder and rain with you
And grateful too
For sunlight on the garden.'

Louis MacNeice

Monday 16th August 1976 After breakfast I worked with the kids up at Meadowbank on the playschool. It was a gorgeous day. After lunch I cleaned up the cars. Hard work. I ran a solid session at night. I saw Ruth McGlashan. It's still less than a handful of times that I've seen her. I said I'd ask her out on Friday but I feel I should really leave it until the Friday, I mean the Sunday. There's a lot of girls in my life just now. But I feel I'm irresistibly being drawn to her and am struggling to resist the magnetic pull. Nobody could replace Alison but I'm sure Ruth could help me forget her a little. I need to phone Archie Strachan to decide whether to take up a place at St Andrew's University rather than Loughborough.

So We'll Go No More A Roving

So we'll go no more a roving
So late into the night
Though the heart be still as loving
And the moon be still as bright.

For the sword outwears its sheath
And the soul wears out the breast
And the heart must pause to breathe
And love itself have rest.

Though the night was made for loving
And the day returns too soon
Yet we'll go no more a roving
By the light of the moon.

Lord Byron

Wednesday 18th August 1976 It's a funny old world. Apart from the fact it isn't. Although she's been out of my life since last December (other than the lovely congratulatory card she sent after my selection for Montreal) I picked up Alison. We went out together for the evening to celebrate her birthday and my return from the Olympic Games in Canada. We had a few drinks at The Laughing Duck and then a baked potato. Later on we sat together in the car at our old lovers' spot just beyond the entrance to the Hermitage on Braid Road. I dropped her at home. As I was leaving, she began to cry...

Thursday 30th September 1976 The usual morning rota with Dad arriving for a loan of the car at eleven o'clock dropping me off in Edinburgh. I picked up some tickets, shampoo and visited the grants people about me going to Loughborough University next month. In the afternoon I sat in reading listening to some music before visiting Alison with some flowers. I'd heard she was a bit depressed. Come the evening I was on the end of a trouncing in training from Paul. Later I phoned Ruth to see how she was doing.

1977

Age 21

23rd April 1977 I picked up Ruth, I mean Susan Rettie! at 9.30 a.m. We took the puppy (that had been abandoned by two guys in a pub last night) up to Meadowbank and managed to find it a new owner. Alison was there. She gave me a lift back home with it at 10.30 a.m. Later on I won a couple of events at the club championships. In the evening Ruth and I went to see Paint Your Wagon and then a meal. She wasn't allowed to stay the evening. Things are difficult for her at home.

For A Dancer

'..I don't remember losing track of you. You were always dancing in and out of view I must've always thought you'd be around...'

Jackson Browne

Friday 16th December 1977 Last year on this day I used my wee one year job to buy a Triumph Spitfire car which was great fun for the short period of time I had it. Anyway back to the here and now. In the lead up to Christmas Jo and I got in the messages from Safeways. I took Will's car. For once it's going well. I've adjusted the idling speed and the volume of petrol mix going in to the engine so it was ticking over nicely. I couldn't get over the cost of the messages - £16! Ruth's voucher was a God-send.

Since it's the student holidays I've signed on the dole. I played an hour of squash with Coach Walker. After a shower looked in to see Will at the hospital. I brought him some ginger beer. He seems to be doing fine. Well at least all things considered. He was glad to see me. He means everything to me.

Afterwards I looked round to see the physio Denis Davidson. He was steamboats. As was his wife Sarah. She promptly sold me a Charlie Chaplin figure. Well I felt obliged. What could I say! They had an old lawyer friend there too. He was in a similar state. Aye you can take the Christmas spirit tae far!

After a fry-up tea at Oxgangs I drove my sister Anne down to Henderson Row to Andy and Maggie Ross'. Anne was staying overnight. We went via Demarco's Cafe at Tollcross. We stopped off for a wee ice cream. Andy had just sat his finals today so fingers crossed. He's a remarkable bloke doing an Open University degree at his age whilst simultaneously running J & R Glen Highland Bagpipe Makers in the High Street. It would be great to see him pass. I had a half pint at Deacon Brodie's Tavern before going round the corner to collect Jo; Aunt Heather; and Frances from the lapidary club to give them a lift home to Porty.

I'd missed Dad. He'd phoned earlier from abroad. He's back home in a week's time. I managed to speak to his wife on the phone. Over a 7-up and a cracker and cheese I sat and watched a Columbo movie - not like me at all.

A very different sort of day and somewhat happier than that somewhat haunted day with Alison two years ago.

And tomorrow? Well more standard fayre awaits me with Adrian on the Meadowbank track. I'm already steeling myself mentally.

1978

Saturday 3rd June 1978 I had a very easy morning. A little studying. And a gentle walk in Portobello Park half thinking about the afternoon's final half putting it out of my mind. I went back home. I had plenty of brown bread and honey. I then went up to Meadowbank.

It was another lovely day with a slight breeze. With it being the Commonwealth Games Trials the place was absolutely buzzing with excitement. A lot of people were looking forward to the 400 metres final. I felt less pressure than many others and more relaxed than normal. Not being the favourite I felt I had nothing to lose. On times this year both the Jenkins' and Kerr were the favourites for the medals in the quarter. Also as I think I'm an automatic selection for the half mile I just wasn't as nervous as usual. Meanwhile Paul should have a clear road in the 800 metres to confirm his place alongside me in Edmonton.

Although it was a hot day I still warmed up in my blue Adidas wet suit. When racing I like to be warmer than usual plus if you'll excuse the contradiction it's a pretty cool outfit. I felt good doing my strides. I was excited about the race looking forward to it rather than being worried. It was almost as if not having to run twice around the track came as such a bonus that I was taking the quarter in my stride.

There was a big crowd there. It was partly because of the importance of the occasion but helped too by the good weather with several spectators sitting out with their tops off.

Before the race a lot of people wished me well. I ran a practice start round the bend and felt good. As I strolled back to the start there was a little bit of extra motivation. Alison was down to spectate. I hadn't seen her for ages. She was standing behind the fence between the track and the cafe. I looked at her and caught her eye. She smiled and waved. I thought here's a great opportunity to show off in front of her. Let's grab the chance!

I'd drawn lane 3 which is a good lane. David Jenkins was outside me. I decided to resist the temptation to go out too hard. Instead I would aim for even paced splits. Roger was inside of me so I was also aware of him chasing me down too. I got out the blocks very well. I relaxed down the back straight but perhaps let too much of a gap open up. Roger moved past me after only a 100 metres.

I didn't panic. Instead I just maintained my pace allowing him to move ahead patiently biding my time. He'd built up a big lead at 300 metres. But when I put the foot down there was a great response there especially compared to everyone else although in reality they were probably just slowing down with me maintaining the pace. I moved past David 50 metres out. I thought I'd left just too much to catch Roger but drove on nipping the verdict on the line just when he thought he'd won the race.

The response from the whole of Meadowbank was delight at my victory. I don't know if it was the surprise or the excitement of the close finish but I've never felt so popular with lots of people congratulating me seemingly genuinely pleased. Another wee bonus was I equalled the Scottish Native Record. A further bonus was that I didn't feel that tired. Any lactic acid generated was relatively fine and minimal. I'd more or less fully recovered within minutes of the race.

When I got home the household was delighted and quite animated. I travelled out to Oxgangs to see Mum and the family. They had watched the race unfold on telly. Mum said she's never seen Grandpa Willie so pleased and happy especially at defeating David Jenkins whose presence has loomed over the household for years.

Once back home to Portobello I went out late on for an easy 4 mile run on a quiet Portobello Golf Course. With it being a soft summer's evening there were still one or two wee groups out playing golf. After all the excitement of the day it was good to take some quiet time out to reflect on what had just gone before and to truly savour the moment. Such days don't come along often in life. I'm aware of just how special an occasion today was.

I wanted to truly re-imagine the day and capture the moment. And whilst I'm naturally delighted for myself what's more important is the joy it's brought to many others in my life.

After beating Dave Jenkins over a quarter mile in some respects there's a certain poignancy. In a way it feels to me that if not the end of a journey it's the end of a chapter in my life.

Seven years ago as a schoolboy I watched David win the 1971 European Championships in Helsinki. His fantastic win there so motivated me that I went out and organised our very own local championships on the track at Redford Barracks. Forty local kids from around Oxgangs turned out. It also provided the motivation for me to go along to Meadowbank and begin training.

So it's been a long road from when I took these first faltering steps. There was no way I ever thought I might beat him over a quarter mile.

There's also a further natural conclusion too as it's the only time David, Roger and I have all raced one another at the Scottish Championships. We'd all previously won the title twice so I feel my third win brings the curtain down on those seven years of our dominance. We may never all race each other again over the quarter mile.

Later on I sat in and relaxed watching Scotland get beaten 3-1 by Peru. A disaster. Talking of disasters. Paul was beaten by Terry Young. I've said a little prayer for him that the selectors take it as a small blip. Young's perhaps fallen in to a no-man's land as he ran a big personal best but only 1.49.4. Whereas Paul ran it from the front going through 400 metres in 52.2 seconds and blew up allowing Young to make up a lot of ground in the last 150 metres. Paul was just too brave for his own good. The team is announced tomorrow. It will be a nervous 24 hours for Paul. But I'm sure he'll be selected.

Age 22

Thursday 28th September 1978 Sandy Sutherland from The Scotsman and Brian Meek from the Scottish Daily Express had both been trying to get a hold of me to comment on Paul's one year ban from international athletics. Come the evening Ruth and I had a few drinks at the Two Inns and some fun winning some money on the fruit machine. Thereafter to Alison's 21st birthday party. It wasn't up to much…

Age 29

Tuesday 27th May 1986 I've been somewhat undisciplined with my diary, exercise, etc. I've been enjoyably busy putting in a lot of hours at work. I didn't note it in my diary but a week past Sunday we had to get Jill (Fox-Terrier) put to sleep. The poor thing was so unwell, mainly caused by a deterioration in her kidneys. The vet was very good giving her a thorough examination and every chance. At the very end she just laid her lovely wee head on the table. It was very moving. Jo especially will miss her. I'll miss the way she used to perform somersaults whenever I arrived at the door. I was reflecting how she was a link to the past. Whilst reading an old diary I was surprised that I had walked her up Arthurs Seat with Alison.

Memories.

Age 60

Monday 4th September 2017

Alison,

In case you're interested just a heads up to say that the book I mentioned to you 6 months ago has been published. I've attached a link and also one to a 'Scotland on Sunday' newspaper feature on it by the journalist Aidan Smith from this past weekend.

Peter

> And the answer, there was none.
>
> Yet the silence it was deafening.
>
> It said everything.

Tell Me Not Here It Needs Not Saying

'...I played with you 'mid cowslips blowing
When I was six and you were four;
When garlands weaving flower-balls throwing
Were pleasures soon to please no more.
Through groves and meads o'er grass and heather
With little playmates to and fro
We wander'd hand in hand together;
But that was sixty years ago.

You grew a lovely roseate maiden
And still our love was strong;
Still with no care our days were laden
They glided joyously along;
And I did love you very dearly
How dearly words want power to show;
I thought your heart was touch'd as nearly;
But that was fifty years ago...'

A. E. Houseman

Printed in Great Britain
by Amazon